HAVE YOU EVER WONDERED . . .

- what the differences between "hard" Science Fiction, "soft" Science Fiction, and "Fantasy" are?
- how to read and understand Science Fiction?
- where the ideas for Science Fiction come from?
- what works are considered the classics of Science Fiction and why?
- where a list of Science Fiction award-winning books and stories can be found?

All of these and a multitude of other questions are answered by L. David Allen in this book. Whether you are an ardent SF reader or are just beginning to savor this fascinating field, his skillful treatment covers the entire spectrum from Jules Verne's 1870 masterpiece, *20,000 Leagues Under the Sea,* to Larry Niven's and Ray Bradbury's latest works. Explore SF, its authors, and critics in this easy-to-read yet highly informative volume.

L. David Allen is currently on the English faculty at the University of Nebraska at Lincoln, where among other duties, he teaches several sections of Science Fiction, a field that he reports is rapidly gaining in popularity and interest. Mr. Allen's enthusiasm for SF began in high school and flourished while he was earning his B.S. at Moorhead State College and his M.A. at Bowling Green State University.

Science Fiction Reader's Guide

by

L. David Allen

CENTENNIAL PRESS

This book was originally published in 1973 under
the title *Science Fiction: An Introduction*.

© Copyright 1973, 1974

by

C. K. Hillegass

First Centennial Press printing 1974
All Rights Reserved

ISBN   0-8220-1611-7

Centennial Press, Lincoln, Nebraska

PRINTED IN THE UNITED STATES OF AMERICA

Contents

Categories of Science Fiction

Although it doesn't really prove anything, and although there are as many dangers to pigeon-holing as there are advantages, it is sometimes helpful to have some kind of categories and subcategories to help one sort things out. It is important to remember that any label emphasizes a single aspect of a work and plays down all the rest of the work; consequently, if such labeling becomes an end in itself, rather than a momentary convenience, the richness and worth of the literary work is virtually destroyed. Furthermore, many sets of labels take no notice of gradations in emphasis, leaving little room for a work that is not purely one thing or another—and most literary works, or anything else for that matter, are not pure anything. Finally, any set of labels can be argued with and rejected by anyone with a different point-of-view. Even with these warnings, it is with some trepidation that the following set of categories for science fiction are offered.

The first category, then, might be called Hard Science Fiction. This would be science fiction in which the major impetus for the exploration which takes place is one of the so-called hard, or physical, sciences, including chemistry, physics, biology, astronomy, geology, and possibly mathematics, as well as the technology associated with, or growing out of, one of those sciences. Such sciences, and consequently any science fiction based on them, assume the existence of an orderly universe whose laws are regular and discoverable.

Under Hard Science Fiction, we can further divide stories into Gadget stories, Extrapolative stories, and Speculative stories. Gadget stories are those in which the main interest is in how some machine, or set of machines, work, or in the development of a machine or other technological device. There are, fortunately, very few of these around any more. Extrapolative stories are those which take current knowledge from one of the sciences and logically project what might be the next steps taken in that science; also included are those stories which take currently accepted knowledge or theory and either apply it in a new context to show its implications or build a world around a particular set of facts. Speculative stories are generally projected farther into the future than Extrapolative stories, and consequently have some difficulty in projecting the logical development of a science; however, the sciences involved in such stories are similar to the sciences we know now and are based in them.

A second general category can be labeled Soft Science Fiction. This encompasses science fiction in which the major impetus for the exploration is one of the so-called soft sciences; that is, sciences focusing on human activities, most of which have not been fully accepted as being as rigorous or as capable of prediction as the physical sciences. Soft Science Fiction would include any stories based on such organized approaches to knowledge as sociology, psychology, anthropology, political science, historiography, theology, linguistics, and some approaches to myth. Stories about any technology related to these would also come under this heading. In this category, as well, the assumption of an orderly universe with regular, discoverable laws is a basic criterion for inclusion. As in Hard Science Fiction, under the category of Soft Science Fiction, we also have Extrapolative stories and Speculative stories; these types are defined in the same way that they were above, with the exception that they deal with "soft" sciences rather than hard.

A third category is Science Fantasy. Under this heading would go those stories which, assuming an orderly universe with regular and discoverable natural laws, propose that the natural laws are different from those we derive from our current sciences. What is sometimes called Paraphysics, but especially those branches dealing with telepathy and the laws of magic, most often provide these alternative laws. To qualify as Science Fantasy, it is necessary that these alternate laws receive at least a minimum of direct exploration.

The naming of the types under Science Fantasy is more difficult. One type might be called Alternative stories, where the underlying natural laws are of a different kind from those we know; telepathy and the laws of magic would belong here. Another type uses scientific information which has been shown incorrect at the time the story was written; it might, perhaps, be called Counter-Science Fantasy. Note that the science current at the time a story is written must be taken into account in classifying, not the science current at the time one reads the story. The third type under Science Fantasy is, perhaps, a branch of Alternative stories, but it has traditionally been identi-

7

fied separately; this is Sword and Sorcery, which is primarily adventure, in which the culture requires the use of swords and other "primitive" weapons rather than modern weapons and, usually, the laws of magic operate in some way. Hopefully, these further subdivisions of what seem to be general categories of science fiction will help to determine what any work is doing and how it relates to other works that are also called science fiction; if they do not, they are worthless.

The final category, Fantasy, is somewhat controversial, for its connection with any of the sciences as such is minimal. Nevertheless, it borders on science fiction and helps round out this system of categories. As the term is used here, Fantasy has much in common with the other categories: it, too, assumes a universe which has order and a set of discoverable natural laws, even though they are different from our own. Unlike Science Fantasy, where these laws are treated explicitly, in Fantasy these laws are merely implicit; if the reader is sufficiently interested, he can formulate the laws governing this fantasy world, but the author gives him little or no assistance.

With these parameters sketched out, it will undoubtedly be helpful to apply them to particular examples. *Conjure Wife,* by Fritz Leiber, is perhaps as pure an example of Alternative Science Fantasy as we have available. That is, it looks at the laws of magic and defines their nature and how they work. Although the main character is a sociologist, this fact is used more as a characterizing device than as an active element in this novel; and although it is suggested that the women involved have psychological problems, these are approached as if their belief in magic and that they are witches are valid, without more than token reference to modern psychology. The only way in which this moves away from the point designated as Alternative Science Fantasy is in the introduction of symbolic logic as a means of bringing various magical formulas into several generalized formulas. However, this does not move it very far toward Hard Science Fiction, since the assumption of discoverable and regular natural law would mean that the scientific method and mathematical manipulation could be used to determine those laws, whether or not they are different from those we know, since they are ways of approaching and working with any kind of regular data.

Another similar example is *The Incomplete Enchanter*, by deCamp and Pratt. It, too, studies the laws of magic, although by a more hit-and-miss method. Symbolic logic is introduced, but here it is used more as a vehicle than as a means of studying magic, so that along this axis the novel would not be quite as far toward Hard Science Fiction. However, along the axis between Science Fantasy and Soft Science Fiction, *The Incomplete Enchanter* would show the distinct difference between it and *Conjure Wife*, for it is more than a little interested in the effects that altered conditions have on people and the way they do things. Finally, this novel slips somewhat toward Sword and Sorcery, since the adventure element is quite strong; it is, however, used more as a vehicle for exploring the other elements than as a point of primary interest.

Most short stories and novels which might be called Counter-Science Fantasy use outdated scientific models in order to do other things more easily. One example of this is Roger Zelazny's "A Rose for Ecclesiastes." This is a very fine story. It belongs here because the portrait of Mars that it uses, particularly the idea that it can support life of a humanoid type and has a thin but breathable air supply, is not consistent with what we now know about Mars—and this was also known when Zelazny wrote the story. However, this is merely a convenience so that the first contact between different cultures, the nature of religions and the bringing of change, the role of language, and several other related points can be explored "purely" —that is, without having to worry about what we know of these things in a definite historical context, without having to worry about what actually did happen on Earth when two cultures met for the first time. The fact that there are a number of plausible technological devices included—spaceships, Mars buggies, etc.—would indicate a slight element of Hard Science Fiction, while the fact that most of the exploration is concerned with religion, psychology, culture and language would move this a long ways up the axis toward Soft Science Fiction. In fact, the only reason that the point of reference is Counter-Science Fantasy is that the outdated model of Mars is necessary before any of the other elements can take form.

It is important to remember that what is known at the time the work was written must be a criterion. For example, much of the information provided about the planets in Asimov's Lucky Starr series is now outdated, and Asimov is among the first to admit it; however, at the time these books were written, that information was based on the best, most current, scientific information available to him. Consequently, these novels would have Hard Science Fiction as their basic reference point, rather than Counter-Science Fantasy.

Rite of Passage, by Alexei Panshin, seems to be largely Extrapolative Soft Science Fiction, since it takes known social institutions, governmental organizations, and psychological patterns, and projects them into an unusual situation. It would, however, be placed somewhat down the axis toward Speculative Hard Science Fiction because the spaceship, the scout ships, the space suits and the faster-than-light travel are basic to the story; they postulate advances in physics that cannot logically be deduced from current knowledge. (It might be noted here that faster-than-light travel is mathematically possible if non-Einsteinian postulates are used; however, at this time what evidence we have tends to support Einstein's theory.)

Frank Herbert's *Dune*, one of the most complex yet well-integrated works of science fiction yet written, seems to be almost equal portions of Hard Science Fiction, Soft Science Fiction, and Science Fantasy in its make-up. The basic reference point is probably Hard Science Fiction, but only because what seems to be the most satisfactory core question deals with the ecology of the planet Arrakis. Among the elements included in this aspect are the elements dealing with the planet, nearly all of which are extrapolated from current knowledge (even the sandworms are probable, based on what we know of Earth organisms of various types). The space travel, the suspensors, the weapon systems, the ornithopter, and various other gadgets also belong in the Hard Science category, although they are speculative rather than extrapolative; they do not make this Gadget science fiction, since little or no emphasis is placed on them in themselves. Those elements which constitute the Soft Science angle include the various approaches to religion, the various approaches to physical and mental training, the Fremen way of life, the political maneuvering on the various scales, Paul's psychological

11

development, and many other related details. Most of these things seem to be based on current knowledge, which is extrapolated and recombined.

The various powers that Paul develops in the course of this book, the powers of his sister, his mother, the Space Guild, and the Bene Gesserit all seem to belong under Alternative Science Fantasy, simply because they deal with things that we have very little information or solid, verified knowledge of. All of these elements are important in the telling of this story, and they are so well integrated that any one of them affects several others directly, and more indirectly. One example of this would be the course of Paul's development: had he not been moved to Arrakis (political), he would not have been confronted by the conditions of the planet (ecology) and thus would not have been under any pressure to develop his trained abilities (soft sciences are involved) nor to develop his natural powers (sight of the future—alternative sciences); in the course of the novel, it is difficult to point to any event, however small, and conclude that only one of these things is present.

The examples are endless, and more and more science fiction is being published every day. Nevertheless, it can be safely generalized that, as the field stands now, nearly every story will contain some combination of two of these categories, and most will be a combination of Hard Science Fiction and Soft Science Fiction, since (historically, at least) science fiction has primarily been interested in tracing the human effects of scientific advances and devices. Of course, when the interest is in such things as the possible workability of magic, then the combination will be between Alternative Science Fantasy and Soft Science Fiction, for a part of the emphasis will still be on the human effects of such advances or changes. Once again, it is the thinking about books and stories that is necessary to put them into such categories that is important, not the categories themselves. At best, categories are stimuli to thinking, helps in determining major functions, and aids in comparing; at worst, they destroy the literary work.

Before leaving this topic, there is one further group of works that border on science fiction that should be mentioned; usually these works are lumped under the heading of New Wave. This is an almost impossible title, for it means something different to almost every individual who uses it. In practice, almost every work which uses science fiction devices, stories, approaches, etc., differently than they have been used in the past is labeled New Wave at some time or another. It is possible, however, to break New Wave into two basic groups; one of these groups is primarily concerned with experimenting with new stylistic techniques within the field of science fiction, while the other group combines such experimentation with the assumption that there is no inherent order in the universe we live in, or at least what order there is is not amenable to study and discover, through the scientific method. Although the first of these groups may provoke the science fiction traditionalists, works which are involved will nevertheless fall into science fiction proper and can be handled by the categories discussed above. The second group, however, should not, at this time at least, be considered as falling within the scope of science fiction, no matter how much similarity there may otherwise be, for this group of works denies the basic premise of science and of science fiction— that is, the assumption that there is an inherent order in the universe and that this order can be discovered through the scientific method and expressed as natural law is absolutely essential, for without this order and this kind of discoverability, science is not possible. This is not to say that this kind of fiction is bad or uninteresting or irrelevant—much of it is very good, very interesting, and very relevant—it is simply not science fiction, but rather constitutes another sub-genre under the general heading of fiction. It is not simply the devices and the conventions that make science fiction what it is; the underlying assumptions, the embodied intent, and the approach to the material are also important.

Analyses of Representative Novels

INTRODUCTION

In the following pages, thirteen science fiction novels representing each of the three main categories of science fiction and combinations of them have been discussed at some length. In addition to these, four other novels and one short story have been discussed in the preceding materials. Choosing seventeen novels from the many good ones available was, of course, difficult and, in many ways, rather arbitrary, though there were some guidelines behind the choices. Historical interest and importance was one of these, particularly in the case of *20,000 Leagues Under the Sea* and *The Time Machine*. In addition, most of those works published after 1952 were winners of awards for excellence; of those that were not, their exemplification of a particular approach to science fiction was an important factor. Finally, the ease with which the works could be found in libraries and bookstores made some difference, though at this writing *The Demolished Man* and *Mission of Gravity* are quite hard to find; their excellence as a type determined their inclusion. Nevertheless, even with these guidelines, choices had to be made, and they were ultimately personal ones.

A few words about the categories of science fiction and the relationships between these works and those categories might be helpful in placing the novels discussed in some sort of overall perspective. In addition, a few comments about A. Merritt, whose best and most important works have been virtually impossible to find at this time, can be made to complement Verne and Wells.

Jules Verne is quite clearly the first writer for whom the wonders of science and scientific discovery as they stood during his time were sufficient in themselves. *20,000 Leagues Under the Sea* is probably his best novel; it is certainly his most popular. In this novel, and in many of his others, he was quite careful to include only those things which were possible according to scientific knowledge and theory of his own time; a large portion of this was accepted as scientific fact in 1870. Because of this, Verne can be said to be the archetypal practitioner of Extrapolative Hard Science Fiction. Hal Clement is probably the best and most consistent descendent from Verne; as noted, there are very few elements of speculative science involved in *Mission of Gravity*, and these are part of the background. As a matter of fact, such elements may be necessary in the modern practice of Extrapolative Hard Science Fiction, for there are few areas on Earth that remain as full of exciting possibilities as the sea was in Verne's time, but we have yet to invent the means of getting to other places in the universe where these wonders and possibilities and applications still exist.

The Time Machine was Wells' first novel, and one of his best. With it, the divergence from the "school" of science fiction headed by Verne was clearly marked. In it, science was used to make possible an exploration

16

of the results of the trends in the social system of the time. The science was imaginary and speculative, though it sounded plausible, but the sociology was extrapolated from trends of the times according to accepted means of interpreting society. Thus, Wells can be said to be the archetypal practitioner of Extrapolative Soft Science Fiction. Many of the novels discussed here show definite relationships with this approach, but *Rite of Passage* seems to be the one which is closest to Wells' practice in *The Time Machine*. It, too, uses an imaginary, speculative science to create a situation in which social and psychological developments and changes can be observed, although the bases for the extrapolations are not always as easy to illustrate as they are in Wells.

Two kinds of writing seem to be related to A. Merritt's work, for whereas Verne viewed the unexplored places on Earth as a scientific gold mine, A. Merritt viewed them as possible resting places for greater beings than man. In many of his stories, particularly in his best novel, *The Moon Pool* (1919), he is concerned with the conflict between good and evil, between light and darkness. Some of his creatures of evil are totally repulsive, even from the printed page, while some of his creatures of good verge on the awe-inspiring. When these aspects of his work are applied to other stories, the result is the tale of supernatural horror, such as those written by H. P. Lovecraft. However, Merritt's work is not primarily horror stories, though there are definite elements of horror in them, for an element of science is also present. In *The Moon Pool*, for example, the main character is a scientist on a scientific mission; he discovers the remains of a much older civilization and becomes enmeshed with it. Furthermore, although they are not given the most prominent place in his work, most of the phenomena encountered have discoverable causes and results. Because these elements are also present, it seems reasonable to consider A. Merritt as the archetypal practitioner of Science Fantasy. *Conjure Wife* is probably the work discussed in this study that is closest to *The Moon Pool,* though there are significant differences between them. Much of the action of *The Moon Pool* takes place below ground, in the ancient kingdom, while *Conjure Wife* makes a point of remaining within the everyday world. Nevertheless, the attitude and the intent of these two works is very much alike.

The other novels discussed here are mixtures of Hard Science Fiction and Soft Science Fiction, for the most part, with the proportion of each fluctuating from work to work. In some of them, such as *Dune,* there may also be a strong element of Science Fantasy included. All of them, however, are excellent reading, and there should be something here to meet nearly any taste among potential readers of science fiction.

Extended analyses of these works is, of course, impossible to do briefly. Consequently, these discussions are intended to be suggestive rather than definitive, to touch on some of those points which are basic to understanding the book and on some of the more interesting aspects of the development of the motivating idea. As a result, the approach taken to each book and the kinds of materials discussed have been determined largely by the books themselves rather than by any consistent critical format. It is hoped, then, that these discussions can provide a basic guide for choosing books to read, a help in reading them, and a stimulus to discussion and further thought about them.

20,000 LEAGUES UNDER THE SEA

Jules Verne

1870

It is easy enough to understand why this novel was received with such enthusiasm when it was first published, for it seems to have introduced many readers to a new kind of world, one which most of them would have had little opportunity to have known very much about at all. And although this novel probably cannot be said to be the first science fiction novel, it did approach its topic in a way that had not been taken before, for everything that Verne included here was valid according to the scientific knowledge and theory current in 1870. It is this last quality, and the character of Captain Nemo, that makes *20,000 Leagues Under the Sea* important in the history of science fiction: it is the first example of strict hard science fiction. Certainly, the novel has lost much of the sense of wonder that it once possessed; the documentary films of Jacques Cousteau have done much to bring the wonders of the underwater world into the living rooms of millions of people in the 1970s, just as Jules Verne did one hundred years earlier. (It is interesting to note that these two Frenchmen have probably done more to stimulate the study of the sea than anyone else.) Thus, although it lacks some of the staying power that most of the work of H. G. Wells has had, *20,000 Leagues Under the Sea* is one of the classics of science fiction.

The story begins when Professor Aronnax, his servant Conseil, and the harpooner Ned Land are swept overboard from the *Abraham Lincoln,* which was commissioned by the United States government to hunt a large "thing" in the sea, which various opinions had thought to be an island, a mechanical marvel, and a previously unknown, unusually large cetacean, with Aronnax holding the latter opinion. Just before these members of the expedition aboard the *Abraham Lincoln* had been thrown overboard, however, they had learned that this was in error and that it was instead a man-made machine. After floating about, they drift up against this marvel. Shortly thereafter, it begins to submerge, taking them with it; however, it stops in time and they are rather roughly brought on board and placed in a dark room for a time. Eventually they meet the captain of the vessel, Captain Nemo; he informs them that he has broken all ties with land, existing only on what the sea provides. His choice, he proclaims, is either to kill them or to keep them aboard with him until they die, for he wants no one to know about himself and his vessel. Fortunately for them, he decides that he will take them along with him on his voyages around the world under the sea.

From this point on, the main action of the story is movement from place to place in the world and the incidents, accidents, and adventures that happen in some of those places. When they are initially picked up they are some two hundred miles off the coast of Japan; by the time they finally escape they have travelled twenty thousand leagues in this ship, ending near the Lofoten Islands off the coast of Norway. For a good while after they are picked up, however, much of their attention focuses on the ship itself and on the marvels to be seen outside their windows. The first notable event is a trip through an underwater "forest" off the Isle of Crespo. During this excursion, they kill a sea otter and a large albatross diving toward the surface, as well as barely escaping the notice of a couple of sharks. From here, their journey takes them toward the Indian Ocean; passing through the Torres Straits, however, the *Nautilus* is caught on a reef. While they are waiting for the higher tide that comes with full moon, Aronnax, Conseil, and Ned are able to once more spend some time on land, exploring and hunting. On their final visit, however, they are attacked by savages, who chase them back to the boat and, next morning, explore the outsides, waiting for someone to come out. They even try to enter, but electric shock holds them off and they retreat, just in time for the *Nautilus* to resume its journey. Following this, there is an incident with another ship, during which Aronnax, Conseil, and Ned are kept locked up, until Aronnax is asked to treat a wounded sailor.

The next stop is for an expedition out of the ship to a large coral growth, an area which Captain Nemo has made into a graveyard for fallen comrades. Later, they visit the pearl fisheries off Ceylon, where they see a gigantic pearl, Captain Nemo's private treasure; during this excursion, Ned Land saves Captain Nemo from a shark after Captain Nemo saves a pearl diver.

They then pass through the Red Sea and pass the Mediterranean through an underground tunnel known only to Captain Nemo (who, after all, has the only working submarine in the world). They cruise through, stopping eventually so that the Professor and Captain Nemo can visit the underwater remains of the lost continent of Atlantis; shortly thereafter, they stop to replenish their sodium supplies from an extinct volcano. They pass then under the Sargasso Sea and test the depths of the Atlantic Ocean on their way to the South Pole, where they spend a good deal of time working their way under the ice to the Pole itself. On their way out, they have a good deal of difficulty, with ice blocking their path in every direction; they barely make it to a spot where they can easily break through the ice in time to renew their air supply, which had nearly run out. From there they go around South America, just by-passing the Caribbean; in the waters off the West Indies, they run into a "school" of giant squid with twenty-five-foot bodies and forty-foot tenacles. A bloody battle follows, which ends with the squids dismantled and fleeing. The ship heads north, passing the coast of Nova Scotia and heads for the British Isles. Just off the coast of Ireland, the *Nautilus* engages another ship in battle, sinking it easily. They continue north; the prisoners decide to escape, doing so just before the *Nautilus* hits the maelstrom between the Vaerö and Lofoten Islands; they are caught in it, at which point the Professor hits his head against the boat and is knocked unconscious; the next thing he knows, he is in a fisherman's cottage on one of the Lofoten Islands, waiting for a way home to France and writing this book while he waits.

This voyage has, of course, several purposes: to exhibit the workings and the abilities of the *Nautilus*, to show the reader some of the wonders of the undersea world, and, perhaps, to convince people that there is much that can be learned from the sea. By modern standards there are some problems with the way that this is accomplished. Perhaps the most serious of these is the fact that the story drags. This is caused by the fact that one of Verne's favorite devices for telling the reader about the particular area that they happen to be in is a listing of the kinds of fish that are to be found there, providing technical names, some classification data, and brief descriptions. These lists sometimes continue for several pages and in a number of instances occupy more than half a chapter. There is, of course, some interest in this, but it does impede the movement of the story. There are other instances where this is not quite as true as it is in the case of the fish. For example, the first few chapters are devoted to introducing Professor Aronnax and the controversy about what this strange thing is that has been sighted; in this instance, there is a good deal of learned argument, some scientific lectures that substantiate the arguments, and a bit of background information. However, this is sufficiently varied and paced quickly enough so that, at worst, it becomes amusing and, at best, it remains interesting. Much the same is true of the details of how the submarine works. Although Verne did not invent the submarine, for at least two inventors had unsuccessfully tested submarines at the time this novel was written, he does seem to have looked at their failures and proposed alternative ways around those problems. Even now, when we have had working submarines for quite some time, it remains fascinating to observe Verne's details of the submarine and its workings and how they are developed into a consistent device.

There are also a number of other "lectures." For example, note the history of some of the ships which the men see sunken at the bottom of the ocean, the learned theories about a wide variety of things, a little information about the various places that they visit, the basis on which Captain Nemo decided there must be an underground passage between the Red and Mediterranean seas, the history of the laying of the cross-Atlantic cable, dissertations on ocean depths and temperatures, the nature of coral growths, the ways that pearls are grown: all of these, and more, are among the things that the reader learns in the course of this novel. Each of these things, in itself, is interesting and fascinating, but the sheer bulk of them, particularly in combination with the lists and classifications of fish, is sometimes overwhelming. In addition, most of what we learn about these things often interrupt any action which might be taking place. The best of them, however, do arise naturally in the course of a conversation or during a lull or as a prelude to action, but others decidedly get in the way of other things. All this makes the novel somewhat easier to read these things, though, if one stops to consider just what it was that Verne seems to be doing in this novel. Perhaps a step back to look at the different ways in which this story of an underwater voyage could have been handled will help to make this clearer.

Basically, there are three ways of approaching this novel. One of these is obviously Verne's, which we shall return to in a moment. A second way might be called a Wellsian approach. That is, this technique would produce a novel in which the scientific theory was still present, but it would be less important, with the main emphasis on Captain Nemo and his quarrel with mankind—a quarrel that has driven him to the solitude of the sea, a burning sense of injustice in his heart. This would make an interesting novel exhibiting Wells' concern with social situations and interpretations of social phenomena. But it would be a very different novel from the one we have before us. The third approach to this voyage could have been the approach used by A. Merritt in his best work. In some ways, this approach is both closest and furthest from Verne's. Characteristically, Merritt chooses a place on

Earth that little is known about; then he postulates the existence of some means of making contact with earlier races who had superior powers to our own. It is also characteristic of his work that such adventures usually concern the struggle between the forces of good and the forces of evil. And in the very best of his work, there is a plausible-sounding "scientific" explanation of much that happens. From Merritt we can trace two divergent fields of science fiction: science fantasy and the kind of horror story written by such writers as H. P. Lovecraft and Ray Bradbury (though Bradbury has written other sorts of things as well). Perhaps Verne and Merritt are most similar because of their sense of wonder, their reveling in the apparently inexhaustible wonders of the world that we live in. Both of them, it should be noted, explore places that are in some way remote and relatively inaccessible to man. Where they differ, of course, is in the wonders they chose to explore. Merritt employs the supernatural; Verne is more interested in what is theoretically possible, using the methods of science as his guide. Particularly at the time that Verne was writing, science was uncovering many new and wonderful things, things that could be seen with the naked eye. In a sense, then, what Verne is trying to do in *20,000 Leagues Under the Sea* is make the reader a participant in a process of scientific discovery, showing him many things that have already been discovered and suggesting many things that are yet to be discovered. For Verne, science and its discoveries were exciting, and he tried to impart a sense of this to his readers. Consequently, his two major characters are a naturalist and an engineer-turned-naturalist, and his method is to describe things in terms that are as scientific-sounding as possible. As noted before, much of this matter is still interesting, though some of it has become outdated and better methods of presentation have been developed.

One aspect of the novel that will not become outdated quickly is the characters. Many readers believe that Captain Nemo is the most interesting, most memorable character in the novel, and there is a certain justification in this. He is a man of mystery and a man without a country. In the course of the novel, the reader actually finds out very little about him. We do learn that he is obviously a superb engineer and theoretician, for the ship that he sails was planned and built by him. We learn that he is an excellent observer and an experimenter, for he has devised many experiments and ways to conduct them that are superior to the ways that others have done them; in addition, the Professor defers to his judgment a number of times on things within the Professor's area of competence. He is also very wealthy, with much of his current wealth coming from beneath the sea, although he must also have been quite wealthy before this, for he was able to build the *Nautilus* on his own. Note, too, that he now gives much of his wealth to the oppressed of many nations.

Besides his devotion to the sea, Captain Nemo (the name means "no man") is driven by two emotions: he is utterly devoted to his own men who sail the *Nautilus* with him, as is he devoted to the oppressed, but his hatred of governments and oppressors knows no bounds and he will not hesitate to destroy any instrument of theirs. However, the reader never discovers which country he came from nor why he is so bitter about life and the possibility of justice on land, though there is one indication that something happened to his entire family.

26

Captain Nemo is indeed a powerful character, but a case can be made that Conseil, the Professor's man-servant, is perhaps the most delightful and memorable character in the novel. Conseil is phlegmatic, uncomplaining, philosophical about whatever happens to him. He is also totally devoted to the Professor and to the task of classifying the denizens of the natural world. What makes Conseil so memorable and so delightful is difficult to explain, since it is usually a matter of the context that his phlegmatic statements occur within. One example occurs when Conseil, wishing to prevent a ray from escaping, receives an electric shock when he touches it; his first act on regaining consciousness is to classify it according to genus, species, and so forth; it is this kind of incongruity that adds charm and relieves some of the slow pace of the book. The Professor is the epitome of learning, a natural scientist from the Paris Museum of Natural History and an expert on life under the sea. At the opening of the book, he has just completed a visit to the United States, a field trip into Nebraska, when he is invited to accompany the *Abraham Lincoln* on its search for the strange "creature" that has been observed. For the most part, he is quite content to go with Captain Nemo wherever he chooses to go, since this allows him to delve further into his particular interest, to update and revise the materials in his earlier book on undersea life, and to learn a great deal about a number of other things. All in all, he is quite reluctant to leave until just before the actual escape, and becomes quite agitated whenever the subject of escape does arise. And the subject is often discussed, for Ned Land, the Canadian whaler, has not much liking for his confinement, no matter how elegant such a life might be or how many different sights there are to enjoy. He has neither the background nor the inclination to enjoy the things that Conseil and Professor Aronnax find so fascinating. He is an active man, a hunter and a meat-eater on a ship where the possibilities of such pursuits are extremely limited. In a sense, he is responsible for much of the suspense in the novel, for he is always looking for a chance to escape, and the reader wonders when and how he will manage to do so. These four are the only characters that the reader gets to know, though there are others who serve various functions from time to time. Each of them portrays a reasonably common response to life and to the situations which they face; both separately and in their interactions they remain interesting aspects of the novel.

In addition to the enduring interest of the characters, there are several thematic points which also retain our interest. It must be recognized that the major, and almost overwhelming, theme of this novel is the many wonders revealed by science and the joys of such discoveries. Consequently, all other themes are rather minor in the scope of the novel. One of the more prominent of these minor themes deals with the nature of freedom and happiness. For the Professor and Conseil, their stay aboard the *Nautilus* does not really raise this question, for they are well fed, they are healthy, and they have an excellent chance to do the things that most interest them. Ned Land, on the other hand, feels cramped and very much a prisoner, even though he has complete freedom of the ship, for his interests cannot be satisfied on this vessel and he cannot live life the way he thinks it should be lived. The result is that Ned is much more concerned about the question of freedom than the other two men; it is he who brings up the possibility of escape at every instance when there is even the remotest chance that it might succeed—and in some instances when there is almost no chance for successful escape. The Professor, on the other hand, is distraught when such an idea is considered, for he realizes what this situation is doing to Ned and that he really should be thinking about escape, but he also knows that he will never have another opportunity to pursue his studies of undersea life. The result is that he argues with Ned whenever the topic is mentioned, trying to make sure that the situation is exactly right before they try it (this is also partly because the Professor knows Captain Nemo much better than Ned does).

Another of these minor themes that retains interest concerns ecological damage. There are several points, for example, when the Professor indicates the usefulness of certain sea-going animals and the probable results should they be slaughtered in sufficient numbers to prevent their being able to do their appointed task successfully. Not only will this affect other life in the sea, but the Professor projects the possible consequences to humans as well. In addition, Captain Nemo is generally a firm believer in killing only what one needs to kill in order to survive; for example, he lectures Ned about the slaughter of whales and about killing for no other reason than for sport. He, however, is not always consistent, for shortly after this lecture, he leads a slaughter of cachelots in large numbers, saying that they are an unpleasant predator. He also leads the slaughter of the giant squids, but there is reason for that. Finally, the fact that Ned is particularly interested in hunting and killing whenever he gets the chance allows an opportunity for the Professor and Conseil to remonstrate with him about this activity—to no avail. It is not that there is no reason for Ned to hunt, for most often he does consider the idea of food; it is the fact that he becomes somewhat irrational when he finds his prey. Even in 1870 there were men who were aware of what man's activities were doing to the environment and what the results could be; it is a sad commentary on man that the same problems are still with us just over a hundred years later.

THE TIME MACHINE

H. G. Wells

1895

Historically, *The Time Machine* is a very important short novel and is all the more amazing since that it was Wells' first novel. That it appeared in a number of shorter forms over a period of seven years in magazines takes nothing from its achievement. Although a number of other stories written before this concerned men traveling in time, the means for such travel had been trance-like sleeps and other similar devices. In *The Time Machine,* the idea of a mechanical device based on a scientific theory—and built by man—was used for the first time. Furthermore, this novel marks a second important innovation: according to what we know now, in 1973, the theory advanced as the basis for time travel by machine is simply not possible; Wells knew this, but constructed a theory which seems consistent, logical, and plausible so that he could explore the future results of trends he saw developing. This also is a first, for previous science fiction had concentrated much more fully on gadgetry and seldom strayed from the scientific knowledge of the time. If these matters were the only value of *The Time Machine*, however, it would certainly not have remained in print so continuously or in so many editions. In spite of some outdated notions, it is still good reading and it still retains its general plausibility. Not only is this a work which has influenced the history of science fiction, it is an example of writing which, though not great, has withstood the test of time.

One of the interesting aspects of this novel is the way that Wells sets out to create a sense of plausibility; he does this well, and many of the devices that he uses are still used in current science fiction. The novel opens with the Time Traveller (he is never given any other name; this label is a device which helps the reader to accept the "reality" of the tale which follows) telling a group of visitors about his most recent work. The chairs they are sitting in are his invention and are described as considerably more comfortable than ordinary chairs; this detail is a nice touch which adds credence to his ability as an inventor. The guests are a varied lot, though all of them are rather ordinary beings; they are sufficiently intelligent and well-read to follow his arguments, but ordinary enough to be skeptical and to resist the idea that he propounds to them. The fact they they break into his explanation to argue and to inject a note of "what-everybody-knows" helps to make this situation more realistic; that he is able to explain why their objections are invalid also adds to this impression, as does the fact that after a model of the device has been demonstrated they are still skeptical but unable to explain otherwise what has happened.

At this point, because the Time Traveller's explanations have been plausible and because the explanations of the guests seem to be simply attempts to explain something they don't understand, the reader is more ready to accept the Traveller's ideas than the guests are, which is precisely the desired effect. The first chapter is used to create this sense of realism, while the second chapter and the beginning of the third chapter develop the story of what the Time Traveller found in the future. Note, in this connection, that, when the guests arrive the following Thursday (Thursday is an established visiting day, with the guests differing somewhat each week), the host is absent, contrary to his usual custom; when he does return, the state of his clothing and his feet, as well as his abstracted air, gives strong reason to feel that something out of the ordinary has happened. This and the later events which led to his being in this condition provide a sense of realism by mutually reinforcing one another. The primary narrator's description, though brief, of the Time Traveller's voice and expression as he told the story, and the suggestion that hearing it and reading it are two entirely different experiences, adds to the reader's willingness to suspend his disbelief. Other details throughout the story further create this suspension of disbelief. For example, consider the details of the last-minute preparations and of the wear that has occurred in the machine; the two little flowers in the Traveller's pocket that cannot be classified as known species; the Time Traveller's confusion as to what is dream and which is reality; the detail of remembering to remove the controls of the machine; his admissions that many of his interpretations of the situation were faulty; the way he compares things which he has seen with life in England; the narrator's mulling over what he has heard; and the description of the last time the Time Traveller was seen. All of these details work toward giving the entire sequence, both frame and story, an air of authenticity and realism. It is well done and it is effective; small wonder that other writers still use these same devices.

The first two chapters, part of the third, part of the last, and the epilogue are concerned primarily with creating this sense of verisimilitude. The rest of the novel is concerned primarily with the developments in humanity, with the Time Traveller's discoveries in a world more than 800,000 years in the future and his interpretations and reinterpretations of them. The world he finds is a very simple world, apparently. The people are tiny, graceful, very beautiful in a fragile way; their voices are musical. Their lives are spent indolently in games and swimming and sportive dalliance. They are vegetarians; the fruits that compose the bulk of their diet are easily available and plentiful, so that no effort need be spent at growing or harvesting.

It does not take long for the Time Traveller to realize that he has landed in a time when humanity is past its peak and on the wane. These people, the Eloi, have extremely short attention spans. They lack any real concern for others and any real interest in anything outside themselves and their habitual pursuits. Their buildings are magnificent, but are very old, well-worn, and falling into disrepair. At first, this life seems idyllic, though a disappointing end for man. Through a gradually more explicit series of clues, the Time Traveller discovers that mankind has developed in two divergent directions. The Morlocks are nocturnal creatures who live underground in the old system of subways, underground machine rooms, etc. Their skin is exceedingly pale, their hair almost colorless,

33

and their eyes reddish. They are the tenders of the machines and provide the Eloi with many of the things that they need. They also are meat-eaters in a world where the Eloi, or themselves, are very nearly the only sources of meat. The Traveller's reaction against them is extreme, for he finds them repulsive and has the overwhelming urge, alternately, to keep away from them or to kill as many as he can. This reaction, incidentally, is not entirely consistent. For example, when he first arrived, the Eloi ran their hands over him out of mild curiosity, which he accepted with some amusement; when he goes underground the first time, the Morlocks do very much the same thing, but this time he ascribes ulterior motives to them and his reaction is to strike out and try to get away, though he is somewhat more tolerant before he discovers that they are meat-eaters. Furthermore, the Morlocks retain the curiosity, the mechanical ability, and the ability to plan and carry plans to a conclusion, which he seems to value and which he is saddened to find missing in the Eloi. Symbolically, his reaction is more understandable, for the underworld has had a long association in men's minds with various forms of evil. However, the analytical abilities of the Morlocks are usually associated with the concept of light, while emotionality (a major feature of the Eloi) is usually associated with darkness. It is only by ascribing ulterior purposes to the use of these abilities—that is, keeping the Eloi as fatted cattle—that this is constructed into the symbolism of the forces of light and dark.

Such action as there is in this story is motivated by two things, the first being the Traveller's curiosity and desire to see as many things as he can in this world of the future. The other, which provides the most overt action because it brings him into conflict with the

Morlocks, is trying to find his time machine, which the Morlocks have moved. These two matters provide just enough action to keep the plot moving and providing a minimum of suspense. The major focus of the novel, however, is not on the action but rather on the society that has developed and the interpretations that the Time Traveller makes.

Concerning the Traveler's thoughts about this new world, note that the amount of solid data that the Time Traveller discovers is quite minute. He learns the language, describing it as simple, composed mainly of nouns and verbs, and incapable of any kind of abstraction. He learns that the Eloi spend the day indolently, have little concern for their fellows, eat only easily available fruits and vegetables, gather at night to sleep in large groups indoors, and have a great fear of the dark. He learns that the Morlocks are nocturnal, are blinded and confused by light of any kind, eat human flesh, are more persistent than the Eloi, and take care of machinery. He discovers the vast system for ventilating the underground. And he notes the evidences that once there was a great civilization in this place and concludes that this civilization vanished a very long time ago. He learns very few other things that could be called "facts" about this world of the future and its history; nearly all else is speculation and interpretation. What is interesting about this is not so much the paucity of information, but that Wells was satirizing a number of other novels, mostly Utopian, in which the stranger to the new world must listen to long dissertations on every imaginable aspect of the alien society; one of the more well-known of such novels is Edward Bellamy's *Looking Backward, 2000–1887 A.D.* Consider, too, Wells' realism: in a short period of time—eight days in this case—one simply would not have the time and opportunity to learn very much about a society, and, furthermore, most ordinary citizens are rarely able to explain very much about their society at all, but especially when they are as child-like as the Eloi.

Another area of interest concerns the Time Traveller's interpretation of the data that he gathers. To a large extent, modern readers will find this interpretation obsolete. However, as an extrapolation of trends and conditions current at the time the novel was written, especially in relation to the socialist point-of-view that Wells espoused, it is logical. In addition, one need know little of the historical background, for much of what the reader needs to know has been provided for him. Thus, the underground existence of the Morlocks is traced back to what the Time Traveller believes to be a rapidly growing trend in his own time (which is Wells' time) to build subways and underground workrooms, to put some of the less attractive aspects of life underground, while reserving the space aboveground for the more ornamental aspects of life and society. Furthermore, he postulates that the beginnings of the distinctions between Eloi and Morlock are to be found in the distinctions between Capital and Labor in his own time, distinctions he believes to be rapidly growing greater. It is logical that, if more of the machinery to support life were to be put underground, the workers would spend a large portion of their time underground; it does not seem impossible, given those trends, that eventually most of their lives would thus be spent underground. Of course, we know now, in retrospect, that this is not the path these developments have taken; nevertheless, what Wells suggested was a logical possibility.

Still another aspect of the Time Traveller's interpretation concerns how this divided-society situation came to be; he provides a historical application of Social Darwinism, which in turn was a sociological application of Darwinian biology. Although Social Darwinism—the survival of the fittest to meet the conditions of society—is no longer accepted as a valid approach to sociology, (even Darwinian biology is still challenged), if we accept its premises, which had great currency in England and America at the time this novel was written, then the projected history is logical. It might be noted here that Wells was a biologist who had studied under Thomas Henry Huxley, a prominent biologist and a primary proponent of Darwinism from the time that *The Origin of Species* first appeared.

If the sociological examination is no longer particularly valid, the situation that is pictured seems to be psychologically pertinent. On this level, which Wells dealt with better than he seems to have realized, *The Time Machine* still has thematic relevance. The split between two dominant approaches to life is still a possibility. In our own time, for example, we can observe a revolt against an entire complex of behavior, a turning from the rational, conscious aspects of mind in favor of a greater appreciation of the emotions and the less conscious aspects of the mind. Furthermore, in the history of the arts, it is easy to trace the alternation of these two approaches to life. Also, there is a long history of man's using dark and light to symbolize the two sides of the human mind; most frequently, there is the indication that the two aspects should be united in a totality, but even this recognizes the possibility of a dominance of one attitude. As indicated earlier, however, the terms of this symbolism as used by Wells do not follow the traditional terms in all respects. To a large extent, the Morlocks do follow these traditional terms as representatives of the darker side of human nature, especially in their avoiding light, their furtiveness, and their cannibalism.

Because Wells views these beings as "thinkers," or at least such thinkers as there are in that world of the future—the ones who run the machines—he suggests several interesting possibilities. The Morlocks possibly represent a basic, perhaps hidden, distrust of machines and of the role that machines play in life. They also suggest a distrust of the rational thought processes of a scientific and technological society. And finally, which is strange in an avowed and lifelong socialist, this portrait of the Morlocks suggests a distrust of the working man who runs the machines. Perhaps, however, this conclusion is too strong; what we are viewing is an end result of a long process. It might be more accurate to say that what is to be feared is the possibility that the machines may control mankind and those men who allow the machines to dictate the conditions of their life.

Objectively, the Eloi are not much of an ideal either, for, although they are lovable and happy, they are also mindless, amoral, and totally dependent on others and on nature for their existence. The Time Traveller does realize this, but when he feels he must make a choice between these alternatives, he chooses those who are most unlike himself, the Eloi. To say that he makes this choice on the basis of his Social Darwinism is, at least partially, an error, for both groups have adapted to their environment; in addition, the Morlocks finally prove that they have an ability to adapt to changing conditions. Furthermore, he recognizes that the sins of the wealthy are earning their just rewards in this reversal of situations. Yet he chooses, and is emotionally aligned with, the Eloi. However, there are still two further factors to be considered. There are suggestions throughout that the Time Traveller feels his own time to be preferable to this future world to come, because of its vigor and its sense of purpose. Yet when he returns, he feels the need to leave again. If the primary narrator's analysis is correct, what he, and the Time Traveller, would like is a simplified age, with mankind's problems solved, but man remaining man as we know him. In a sense, this is a plea for psychological wholeness, for a union rather than a split between the aspects of the human mind. On another level, it is a dream which one may quest after but never find, either in the present or in the far future. This entire level of psychological dualism in the novel is quite complex; it leaves no certain answers, no certain interpretations. Instead, it raises a host of questions to be pondered. More than any other aspect of the novel, it seems to be this aspect which is responsible for the continued popularity of *The Time Machine*.

If this were the only work that Wells had ever written, he would still deserve a place of honor in the history of science fiction. This novel is the first time machine story. More than that, however, it is the first example of what we can call extrapolative soft science fiction. That is, it uses a science—in this case imaginary—to create a situation in which changes in human society can be presented, explored, and interpreted by extending trends current at the time it was written. That is does this convincingly and well, and that it is solidly and competently written, are additional virtues that assure its place and give it continuing influence.

This, of course, is not all that Wells did, for his was a remarkably fertile imagination, particularly in the earlier years of his writing. Since he initiated them, many of his ideas have been used again and again; some have been improved upon, while others have become clichéd and degraded, yet Wells dealt with these things seriously and credibly. Wells also originated some other ideas that have not fared quite so badly, although the quality of succeeding uses has varied. He was the first to use the theme of conquest from space (*The War of the Worlds*), the idea of interplanetary television ("The Crystal Egg"), and the possibility of a collision between Earth and a body wandering in space ("The Star"). Wells' *The Invisible Man* is still one of the better explorations of invisibility, while *The First Men in the Moon* presented a plausible way for men to reach the moon, explore it, and return to Earth. The list of Wells' innovations is enormous; though the quality of the writing is uneven, these ideas are nearly always treated in the same careful way that the ideas are treated in *The Time Machine*. It is his treatment of ideas, as well as the ideas themselves, on which the continuing reputation of H. G. Wells rests.

I, ROBOT

Isaac Asimov

1950

This is one of the two works for which Isaac Asimov is most noted, the other being the Foundation Trilogy. It is not a novel, but rather a closely connected sequence of short stories within a frame. Together, these stories trace the development of robots from rather crude machines through increasing sophistication to the ultimate hope for mankind. The vision involved in this projection may be faulty, especially since dates were given for many of the developments, but what makes this work both fascinating and important is the development of the three laws of robotics, which have influenced nearly every novel or short story dealing with robots that has been written since this volume was published. They have also made such stories much more believable and interesting, as well as providing a baseline against which a writer can operate and expand beyond; in short, Asimov's laws have become one of the conventions of science fiction, and this is the work in which they figure most fully, although he has written others using them.

The frame-story concerns Susan Calvin, who joined U.S. Robots in 2008, just twelve years after the first robot was made and sold. She was a robopsychologist, the first worker in a new science; primarily, the robopsychologist helps to set the possible variables within the robot brain so that the robot's reaction to specific stimuli can be accurately predicted and, if something should not go as predicted, to figure out what the problem is and how it can be handled. She is a master at this new science, but she is also a rather crusty soul, much more at home with robots than with people and not very tolerant of anyone who is either lazy or stupid. She is a caricature of the so-called female Ph.D. as they were believed to behave in the 1940s, when most of these stories were written. The story of Susan Calvin is an excellent choice for this frame, for not only has her career paralleled the growth and development of the robotics industry, but she also knows the important incidents thoroughly and can pass them on, through the reporter who is interviewing her. Some of the stories include her as a character, but others do not; this, of course, does not matter, since they involve aspects of robot behavior that she would have learned about through reports and by talking with the characters involved. In short, she lends an authoritative voice to the larger story of the development of robots, in addition to being a rather delightful character in her own right.

The first story, "Robbie," takes place before Susan Calvin joined U.S. Robots, in 1998. However, she is present in the story as a girl in her mid-teens, observing the first talking robot and listening to the questions that people ask it; this aspect is covered in five sentences and has almost nothing to do with this story as such. There are, however, two major emphases in this story: the nature and function of the first robots sold, and the human reactions to robots. Robbie is a nursemaid, a rather large robot who moves with a sort of rhythmic thump and who has a head and body that are parallelepipeds with rounded edges connected by a rather thin stalk of flexible metal. His eyes are glowing red and his shoulders flat; all told, he is not particularly aesthetic. However, as a nursemaid, he is excellent, for he can do all the things a human companion can do, except talk, and he has much greater patience. Furthermore, his reaction time is quicker and he can move much faster than any human companion could in an emergency. Thus Robbie is an excellent companion for a child. The story is built, of course, around the human reactions to Robbie. Gloria, the eight-year-old girl whose companion he is, loves him in much the same way that she would love a pet, though possibly more because he can play with her in more satisfactory ways than a pet could. Her father views him in terms of cost and functionality and is generally well satisfied with his investment. But her mother reacts emotionally against Robbie; to her, he is a terrible machine that has no soul and that might go berserk if a part were to jiggle loose. She also believes that children weren't made to be guarded by ugly metal things. Her view seems to be shared by a large number of the other people living around them. Consequently, she campaigns to get rid of Robbie and eventually succeeds; the way she reveals this to Gloria is interesting, for it suggests that she does not understand human beings either. Gloria's reaction is intense; nothing, she says, will take Robbie's place. Finally, her father arranges to have them take a tour of U.S. Robots and Mechanical Men, where she and Robbie will meet again; this meeting is more dramatic than he had planned on, for Robbie alone reacts fast enough to save her life when she moves into the path of a huge tractor. This is enough to bring her mother to some acceptance, however reluctant, and Gloria gets to keep Robbie. In terms of the book as a whole, this story gives the reader a favorable view of robots and a rather unfavorable view of people like Mrs. Weston, who oppose robots on purely emotional grounds. We are also given a portrait in some depth of the first robots made and sold, against which later developments can be measured, as well as a much briefer view of the first talking robot, an exhibition piece whose repertoire is very limited.

Within the setting of the second story, "Runaround," people like Gloria's mother have forced world governments to ban robots from Earth except for purposes of research, a stand which had both economic and religious backing for its goals and which took on strength as robots started to look more human. By that time, however, off-planet markets had begun to open up, so that U.S. Robots had some reason to continue to develop new types.

"Runaround," as well as the two stories following it, "Reason" and "Catch That Rabbit," have as their main characters Mike Donovan and Gregory Powell, men who were the primary troubleshooters for U.S. Robots during those early years. In each case, the robots are acting strangely and the job of Donovan and Powell is to find the reason and remedy the situation. Furthermore, each of these three stories is a good example of the use of the scientific method, though "Reason" gives it a somewhat different twist. In "Runaround," the robot Speedy (for SPD 13) has been sent onto the surface of Mercury to gather selenium; contrary to expectations, however, he has been gone for five hours and his course for the previous two hours has been a constant circle around a pool of selenium. Powell and Donovan must use older-style robots from the first expedition to go onto the surface in suits that allow them only twenty minutes in the sun to try and stop Speedy and bring him back. As they travel, and just after they get there, they gather the information that they have; when they find Speedy, they find him acting as though he were drunk, which suggests that there may be some conflict between two of the laws of robotics. That is, Speedy has been given an order by a human which he must obey (2nd law), but it was given no particular urgency so that the 3rd law (protecting his own existence when it does not conflict with the 1st or 2nd laws) dominates; he is unable to choose between them and consequently circles the pool where he has been sent—but where he senses danger. Once they have

44

determined this, they must also determine what the danger is and how to get him out of there; they do find a workable method, but they do not have sufficient material to make it work long enough to do the job. Finally, Powell invokes the first rule (protecting human life), just barely getting Speedy to rescue him before the glare of the sun destroys him.

"Catch That Rabbit" is a similar story. The problem with Dave (for DV-5), who is designed to direct six other robots, is that he seems to work smoothly but the team does not produce any ore, as they should, unless there is a human being present, which shouldn't be necessary. The question, of course, becomes how to find out what is wrong if one can't watch it happen. Once again, a number of tests are run, a number of possibilities considered and rejected, and finally several other ideas are tried out, ending, of course, with the right one. The real problem is that, somehow, during emergency situations, the strain of giving orders to six other robots causes Dave to develop somewhat of a short circuit and, in effect, twiddle his thumbs instead of facing the crisis squarely. Once one of the other robots has been removed, there is no longer a problem. Both of these stories follow a definite order: first the problem is discovered, then as many facts as possible are gathered and evaluated, which in turn provides a theory of what is wrong, which provides a basis for a set of predictions about what might solve the initial problem, and finally these predictions are tested to find out whether they are correct or incorrect. If they are incorrect, they must refer back to some point in this process, correct their information and theory, and try again. This process is the scientific method, which gives Donovan and Powell a method for approaching the problems they face in an orderly fashion. There is a suggestion that they are the top troubleshooters precisely because they apply the scientific method so carefully and thoroughly, but also with a healthy respect for intuition.

In "Reason," this rational approach to information concerns not Donovan and Powell but Cutie (for QT-1), a robot built in space to run the Converter, which focuses energy beams to receiving stations on Earth. His major feature is an extremely high logical faculty and a demand for empirical data. He uses the faculty and the data he has available to him, using logical processes and the scientific method to construct a theory of why he exists, much as Descartes did in human terms; his ultimate result is that the Converter is the Master and that all must serve Him. Since Donovan and Powell are the only humans he has had contact with, and since his only experience of the universe outside the station has been through the instruments in the station, it is rational and logical to reject any of the explanations that the humans may provide for his existence or the function of the Converter. This is extremely frustrating for Donovan and Powell, but they discover that Cutie handles the functions he was designed to handle perfectly and decide that the question of his beliefs is irrelevant. Thus, where "Runaround" and "Catch That Rabbit" show the positive possibilities of the scientific method, "Reason" shows that the results of using it are only as good as the data they are based on; there is nothing in the scientific method that guarantees the correctness of the facts or that correct results may not be reached by the wrong means.

In a sense, the next story, "Liar!" is a much more human story. That is, although the main focus in the Powell and Donovan stories is on the two men themselves, it investigates their trying to find out something about robots; here, however, we look directly at the hopes and inner motivations of several characters, including Susan Calvin, and at some of the consequences in human terms. The robot of this story is Herbie (for RB-34). Through some fluke of the manufacturing process, Herbie is a mind reader. Because the first law of robotics requires that robots not injure human beings or allow them to come to harm by not acting, Herbie feels that he must tell people the things that they would like to hear. Thus, he tells Susan Calvin that a young man whom she admires is in love with her, which is not true but is what she would like to hear. He tells both Dr. Lanning and Peter Bogert that their mutually contradictory mathematics are correct. He tells Bogert that Lanning has already resigned and that he will be the next director. All of these characters act upon this information, and, because they want to hear these things, they don't stop to question them or the source. However, once they discover that they have been told things that are not true, it does not take long to figure out why Herbie told them these things, and it does not take Susan Calvin long to render Herbie inoperative by confronting him with a dilemma which cannot be solved: it hurts to be told the truth, but it also hurts *not* to be told the truth. And this, of course, is the point of the story.

"Little Lost Robot" demonstrates the application of the scientific method to a mystery. These robots, Nestor-10s (NS-10), have been modified under pressure by the government so that a research project might proceed post-haste; the modification is the removal of that part of the first law which directs robots not to allow humans to be injured, for the project requires that men expose themselves for short periods to gamma radiation, and unmodified robots both got in the way and ruined themselves by exposure. The robot of the title, one of the modifieds, had been told by one of the humans to get lost; he does so by joining sixty-two identical robots; thus, Susan Calvin and Peter Bogert must be transported from Earth to find him, since now there are sixty-three robots of the same type on the base. Dr. Calvin's first steps are to consider the various implications that the change in the first law could have, one of which is that such a robot could develop a superiority complex and act on it. She then proceeds to find out as much of the background situation as she can, after which she interviews each of the sixty-three robots. When that fails, she discusses other possible tactics with Bogert. As further information is available, she creates situations in which to test some of her predictions, but these are no help since the robot is very intelligent and has been able to convince the other robots that certain actions would be foolish. Finally, they realize the one difference between the lost robot and the others—the ability to detect gamma radiation, testing that prediction, and thus finding the robot. This is a most interesting story, and it is fascinating to watch the interplay of personalities. However, the main point of the story is the function of the three laws of robotics and the importance of each aspect of those laws.

"Escape" brings Donovan, Powell, and Susan Calvin together again, relating a story of how a computer brain with an impressed personality at the level of a child finally solves the problem of interstellar travel. The inter-company rivalries, the way that Susan Calvin manages the Brain and the information to get results, the tricks that the Brain plays on Donovan and Powell, the personality of the Brain, and the fact that mankind finally finds its way out of the solar system—all of these things make this story good reading. However, in terms of the book as a whole, possibly the most significant fact is that the story, for the first time since "Robbie," takes place mainly on Earth, that the lessons in robopsychology that have been learned from increasingly sophisticated robots working in various situations in space have been applied on Earth. The laws against robots on Earth are still in effect, but the Brain is technically a computer, and looks like one, and it is also capable of accomplishing things on its own initiative. In this way, the stage is set for the extremely complex computers that, in effect, run the world by the time of the last story in this book.

"Evidence" is another "mystery" story. The question raised is: "is Stephen Byerly a robot?" The question is a part of a political maneuver to keep Byerly from winning the race for mayor in the home city of U.S. Robots, and it is based on several oddities about him, such as the fact that no one has ever seen him eat or sleep. The progress of this political battle is, of course, very interesting in and of itself. However, there is more to the question than that, for it becomes a question of who is more fit to govern, man or machine, especially if the machine has all the available data, the ability to integrate it all, and the desire to use this knowledge for the benefit of all mankind rather than any particular segment. The initial raising of this question lies in this story, but it reaches its culmination in the last story. In "Evidence," however, there is no real solution to the mystery, for everything that is raised to suggest that Byerly is a robot is capable of another interpretation—namely, that he is simply a

49

very good man who is able to live up to an ideal of human conduct; granting that there have been very few men like that, there have nevertheless been enough to make it a possibility. On the other hand, those things which might suggest that he is human are not necessarily conclusive; for example, when he hits a man: if he is a robot, might not his creator have created another robot for him to strike? No answer is ever given, although Susan Calvin believes that he is a robot and her view tends to influence the reader. Furthermore, the fact that she thinks that this is a positive benefit for mankind is also convincing to the reader; at the very least, he is not likely to feel the naked prejudice shown by the reporter in the frame-story that links these separate stories into a larger story.

Finally, in "The Evitable Conflict," we see a vision of a basically united world which seems to be run by men, but which is actually run by the successors of the Brain (from "Escape"). The problem seems to be that some men are trying to lead a revolt against the Machines and thus cause economic disruption that will discredit the Machines. However, Susan Calvin explains to Stephen Byerly, who is now World Coordinator, that not only do the Machines take this into account and correct for it, but also that this is for the good of all mankind—rather than the few, and that the Machines are only superseding, in a more consistent and intelligent way, the forces which have always controlled mankind. Her view of the matter is extremely positive, with an emphasis on the benefits that mankind may gain from this, although such a society is not detailed in any way. Thus what we are left with is the suggestion that not only is this the direction in which man will develop but also that this is the direction in which man *should* develop. It is interesting to note in this connection that some twenty-three years later, Asimov has not changed his opinion to any great extent, for in a recent issue of *Fantasy and Science Fiction,* his regular column details the uses of machines for making the world a better place for humans to live.

Thus, in this book we have several things happening simultaneously. First of all, we have a series of stories, all of which are interesting and enjoyable reading. Second, in a series such as this, these stories project the development of robots from rather crude, slow-thinking giants to, possibly, a humanoid appearance and to machines which are capable of undertaking world-wide planning for mankind. Third, these stories are studied in psychology, both robot and human. Susan Calvin points out in "Evidence," for example, that the three laws of robotics are only a restatement of principles that many of Earth's ethical and religious systems are built upon; consequently, the problems which we see with the robots can be applied to man as well: men often reason from faulty data in the same way that Cutie does in "Reason"; men who are given more responsibility than they can handle react in ways similar to those of Dave in "Catch That Rabbit"; and thus it continues through each of these stories, except perhaps for the last two. Finally, and especially in the last two stories, we are impressed by the benefits that mechanical men and sophisticated computers can provide for mankind—if we can overcome our prejudice against machines and put them to proper use—assuming always that we program them properly in the first place. *I, Robot* is not only a landmark in the development of science fiction, it is also a work which is well worth reading on its own terms, at any time.

THE FOUNDATION TRILOGY

Isaac Asimov

Hugo Award, Best Series, 1966

One of the staples of science fiction, especially in its earlier days, has been that kind of adventure story called the "Space Opera." The term, of course, is derived from its similarity to the "Horse Opera" dealing with stories about the West; replace the horse with a rocket ship, the six-shooter with a ray gun or some other such advanced weapon, the chaps and spurs and boots with a space suit, the moustachioed villain with a Bug-Eyed Monster (BEM for short), and the Old West with a strange planet which we have not yet reached, and the two kinds of stories will not be very different at all. Just as the sweep of the wide open spaces accounts for a part of the popularity of the "Horse Opera," so too is the sense of wonder at the vastness and the possibilities of the universe partly responsible for the appeal of the "Space Opera." There are, however, two main differences. "Space Opera" traditionally places a great deal of emphasis on super-science, on gadgets and devices and weapons that have been produced by sciences that are far advanced. The other difference lies in the fact that the battles with the enemies encountered as mankind penetrates the reaches of space tend to become bigger and more fearsome, as do the weapons, at a geometric rate. Presented in this way, "Space Opera" might seem to be a waste of time, a kind of story that has no business being considered seriously at all. Many of the stories that fall under this heading probably should not be seriously considered, though they can make for enjoyable reading. To dismiss all the stories in this category as worthless, however, would be a mistake, for many interesting ideas and many possibilities of what man might face in the universe have originated in the pages of "Space Opera" and have become important elements within the field of Science Fiction.

What has all this to do with the Foundation trilogy? It provides us with one point from which to measure Asimov's achievement in writing the three novels that make up the trilogy, for the "Space Opera" seems to be the nearest science fictional ancestor of this work. Much of the framework is the same, particularly in the sweep of time and space that these three novels cover. There are also many new and wonderful gadgets in these stories, products of an advanced science and civilization; there is a change here, however, for these gadgets remain largely in the background, most of them taken for granted as parts of the civilization which people have lived with most of their lives. Of course, since these novels span some four hundred years or so, and since they deal with planets at various stages of development, there are new devices developed in the course of things, some of them quite useful in resolving some of the conflicts that take place; even so, they do not receive the attention that they probably would have received in straight "Space Opera," where their development and workings and effects would be a major focus of a novel or some section of it.

Many "Space Operas" chronicle the rise and fall

of galactic empires; usually the emphasis is on the fall, which is normally brought about by warfare on a huge scale. Here again there is a difference between the traditional story and the Foundation trilogy, for Asimov concentrates on the fall and rise of an empire, focusing on the rising of a new empire out of the ashes of the old. Furthermore, instead of viewing this process either on a broad, general scale where humans are virtually ignored as individuals or on the plane of the mechanical forces which are brought to bear in the destruction of a civilization, Asimov uses individual human beings who have played a role in some pivotal event in the history being made; we, as readers, see the social situation largely through the eyes of these individuals, as we also see the events in which they are involved. And although these characters are all heroic in the sense that they are agents who bring about significant changes in their society, the reader comes to know them as individuals with strengths and weaknesses, rather than simply having to accept only heroic qualities on a remote level. Finally, Asimov shifted the entire focus from the physical sciences to the social sciences. This is not to say that physical science is ignored in these novels, for it does play an important role and it is accurate within the limits of the time at which they were written. However, the major scientific advance postulated in this trilogy is the development of psychohistory; this development is made possible by the fact that mankind has reached sufficient numbers by the time of the stories that the Uncertainty Principle can quite accurately predict what will happen under certain sets of circumstances, in much the same way that we can make predictions about atomic theories today. Furthermore, the emphasis in these novels is on people and their societies and the means by which they cope with the various crises that they face. Any one of these modifications would represent a significant achievement; that Asimov has accomplished all of these things, and in a literate and extremely readable fashion, emphasizes this achievement and explains why the Foundation trilogy merits the Hugo awarded it as the best all-time series.

In a sense, the Foundation trilogy should not be considered a trilogy at all, for it is composed of nine different stories published in three volumes. On the other hand, those stories included in *Foundation,* the first volume of the series, all deal with the beginning of Hari Seldon's plan and with the smooth workings of his predictions; the stories in *Foundation and Empire,* the second in the series, deal with the middle period and with the unpredictable appearance of a powerful mutant, the Mule, thus marking the pivotal point where the plan and the predictions can go awry; in *Second Foundation,* the search for the Second Foundation that Seldon was supposed to have established to watch over the first, and the misdirected successes which allow the citizens of the First Foundation to return to the path of the prediction, are emphasized. Perhaps at this point it would be helpful to have a brief overview of the stories, the major characters and the events in them, and the relative time scheme involved. The dates are given in Foundational Era (F.E.) notation; 1 F.E. is approximately the year 12,069 of the Galactic Era; the number of years from the present until the time that man moved beyond the solar system into the galaxy to inaugurate the Galactic Era is not suggested.

FOUNDATION

Part I "The Psychohistorians"

— 2 F.E. Hari Seldon, the originator of psychohistory and the founder of the two foundations, and Gaal Dornick, a new assistant to Seldon who recently arrived on the Empirial capital world of Trantor, are the two major characters. The story deals with the reaction of the court to Seldon's predictions and the way in which he manipulates the government into supporting the First Foundation, the only official one, on a remote world.

Part II "The Encyclopedists"

Approximately 50 F.E. Lewis Pirenne, the director of the Foundation's Encyclopedia project on Terminus and consequently the highest authority on the planet, and Salvor Hardin, Mayor of Terminus City, are the main characters. The story focuses on the attempted annexation of Terminus by the Kingdom of Anacreon which Salvor Hardin averts, and in the process, he supercedes the Encyclopedists as the central authority; in showing this first crisis, the story also shows, indirectly, the deterioration of the Empire.

Part III "The Mayors"

Approximately 80 F.E. Once again Salvor Hardin is a main character; his primary opposition is Prince Regent Wienis of Anacreon. The story deals with the second crisis of the First Foundation, another attempt to annex Terminus to Anacreon which is thwarted by the use of a "religious" power established after the first attempt.

Part IV "The Traders"

Approximately 135 F.E. Limmar Ponyets, an independent trader, and Eskel Gorov, Master Trader and agent of the Foundation, are the main characters. The Foundation has been spreading its influence, using a priesthood of engineers as a necessary part of its assistance to other worlds; in this story, Gorov has been imprisoned on a planet which refuses to accept either the atomics which the Foundation is peddling or the "religion" which goes with them, so Ponyets manages both the rescue and the introduction of the atomics into the society, though without the religion.

Part V "The Merchant Princes"

Approximately 155 F.E. Jorane Sutt, secretary to the Mayor of Terminus, Hober Mallow, Master Trader of Smyrno, and Commdor Asper Argo, ruler of the Korellian Republic, are the central figures in this story in which an attempted war by Korell against the Foundation is halted by establishing trade and in which the Mayorality passes into a plutocracy of the merchant princes.

FOUNDATION AND EMPIRE
Part I "The General"

Approximately 195 F.E. As befits a longer story, the cast of characters is longer here: General Bel Riose, a young, ambitious, first-rate general of the Empire; Cleon II, the Emperor; Brodrig, his most trusted advisor; Lathan Devers, a trader of the Foundation who is "captured" by the General's forces; and Ducem Barr, a patrician of Siwenna, a long-time rebel against the Empire, and the son of a man whom Hober Mallow met in "The Merchant Princes." Picturing the decay of the Empire, this story presents the last confrontation between the Foundation and the Empire, lost by the Empire because the Emperor distrusted his men.

Part II "The Mule"

This section covers a five-year span, approximately 295-300 F.E. Again the cast of characters is larger, including Bayta and Toran Darell, newly-weds who are pressed into the service of trying to find out about the Mule; Captain Han Pritcher, a Foundation Army man who comes under the influence of the Mule; Ebling Mis, the Foundation's foremost scientist; and the Mule, a mutant totally unexpected within the Seldon Plan who conquers the Foundation; Magnifico, a clown and court jester taken in by Bayta and Toran. There are two main sequences to the action: first, there is the process by which the Mule conquers the Foundation; second, there is the search for the Second Foundation, with its disclosure prevented just in time to halt the Mule. Running through both of these is the question of exactly who and what the Mule is.

SECOND FOUNDATION

Part I "Search by the Mule"

Approximately 305 F.E. The Mule and Han Pritcher both reappear in this story, with Bail Channis, a young adventurer who turns out to be a member of the Second Foundation, added as a major character. The Mule once again searches for the Second Foundation; Bail Channis misdirects, unknowingly, this search and thus lures the Mule into a situation where his mind can be adjusted from conquest to consolidation in the five years remaining before his death.

Part II "Search by the Foundation"

Approximately 400 F.E. The characters include Arkady Darell, an adventurous fourteen-year-old girl who is the granddaughter of Bayta and Toran; Dr. Toran Darell, her father, one of the foremost scientists of the Foundation, and a firm believer that the Second Foundation must be eliminated; Pelleas Anthor, an agent of the Second Foundation who manages a large part of the misdirection; Preem Palver, First Speaker of the Second Foundation, who also assists in the misdirection; Stettin, the Mule's successor. The Second Foundation is seen to be manipulating events so that the First Foundation will return to a course that is closer to the original Seldon Plan and will regain at least an illusion that it is guiding its own destiny; the war with Kalgan and the "discovery" of the Second Foundation on Terminus are both parts of the strategy of the Second Foundation.

Clearly, the most fascinating thing about this series of stories is the sweep of history that it portrays; most of the themes that hold these stories together as a series are related to the historical process. However, one of the features that makes the Foundation trilogy such a great achievement is the fact that each of the stories is excellent in itself, with its own themes and perspectives; all of them could stand alone and still be fascinating stories.

Perhaps the most significant of the overall themes in these stories is revealed at the conclusion of the third volume, when Preem Palver is talking to the student; the idea is that a saner way of life may result from the reunion of the two foundations after each has had a thousand years to develop separately at "opposite" ends of the galaxy. The concentration of scientists on Terminus with the First Foundation serves two purposes. First of all, it insures that some-place in the galaxy there will be a world in which education and development in the sciences will con-tinue, despite the political upheaval suffered else-where in the galaxy; instead of being scattered throughout the remnants of the Empire, a large num-ber are together in one spot. Second, it creates a situ-ation in which the physical sciences, but especially physics and the related technology, will have to be developed to a much higher degree than that achieved by Empirial science; the planet on which Seldon plants them is very poor in natural resources and in a very vulnerable spot; thus, the scientists must make both the most efficient use of the materials that they have available to them and the new develop-ments that will allow them to use other materials if they are to survive. In addition, they need some means to hold possible conquerors at bay; the tech-nology which they command, even though it is not a military technology, accomplishes this goal. While the scientists on Terminus are developing the physical sci-ences and honing knowledge of the physical uni-verse, the members of the Second Foundation (where it is located is a mystery to be solved throughout these novels, so I'll not reveal it) have been given the task of perfecting psychohistory and the "human" sciences, especially involving the development of the poten-tials of the human mind. As we see in the last vol-ume of the series, they have moved at least as far in that direction as the physical scientists have moved in theirs. It is, however, apparent in "Search by the Foundation" that a certain amount of time will be necessary before the members of the First Foundation will be capable of accepting the knowledge and abilities offered by the Second Foundation, for they are rather paranoid about the idea of anyone's shaping their future, or even predicting it, especially after the Mule shows that psychohistory is not infallible. The Second Foundation is, of course, aware of this and in the last two stories attempts to create the illusion of self-sufficiency and self-determination for the First Foundation but, at the same time, subtly moves the course of events toward the path predicted by Seldon. Over the first four hundred years after the launching of the Seldon Plan, the First Foundation has steadily widened its sphere of influence in a peaceful manner through its technological abilities, while the Second Foundation has kept watch, developed human potentials, and modified the Seldon Plan according to the precise events that occur; it is implied that over the following six hundred years the First Foundation will continue to spread its influence and create a high level of civilization, thus unifying the galaxy into a loosely-knit empire once again, while the Second Foundation will continue as before while gradually introducing the fruits of its labors unobtrusively, so that when the two foundations finally meet again after a thousand years it will be a reunion rather than a confrontation. The reunion of these developments by both groups should, it is suggested, produce a civilization on a higher level than either of the parts and higher than the civilization that gave rise to them.

Another of the overall themes that unites these nine stories deals with the rise, fall, and change of governments. One thread deals with the fall of the galactic empire which had unified and ruled all the inhabited planets in the galaxy, a task so large that everything was devoted to it. The first story, "The Psychohistorians," portrays Trantor, the capitol world, just before the dissolution of the Empire begins; the people involved are of the last generation who can say that Trantor rules all the inhabited worlds. One of the weaknesses of the Empire is the fact that, except for one hundred square miles for the Imperial Palace, the city covers the planet completely; thus, Trantor, and the rulers of the galaxy, are dependent on others for many of the necessities of life, but especially for food. In addition, the numbers of worlds rebelling against the Empirial rule seem to be increasing; when the number reaches a certain point, not only would the Empirial forces be spread very thinly, decreasing the chances of putting down the revolt, but the flow of supplies could be easily cut, leaving Trantor to face severe shortages. Thus, some worlds would be able to gain a freedom of action; those farthest away from the capitol would be the first to go, with the circle moving farther and farther in. However, the quality of the rulers is likely to decline. It is a common charge today that those in Washington have little realization of what is going on in the rest of the country and take refuge in the forms and technicalities of their jobs; the possibilities of this sort of thing would be immensely magnified in a galactic civilization and its government. The growth of a court surrounding the Empirial leaders would also insulate the rulers from the situations they are governing, create the setting for a variety of intrigues, and institute other means than merit and knowledge for placing people in important positions. Suspicion will be rampant in such situations, with protecting what power one has being a primary motivation at all levels, including the Emperor. All of these things can be clearly seen throughout the Foundation trilogy. Suspicion is rampant, both in the court during Seldon's time and under the reign of Cleon II; in the first case, Seldon is able to manipulate it to gain his ends; in the second, this suspicion actually weakens the Empire, although it strengthens Cleon's position momentarily. In addition, it is the really capable people who suffer from being capable—and thus a threat to the power of the Emperor; Seldon, Bel Riose, and Brodrig are either eliminated or relegated to minor positions away from the seats of power. Siwenna rebels against the Empire because of a corrupt, self-serving Empirial governor; because it is quite close to Trantor, as such distances go, the Siwennese rebellion is put down. However, Anacreon annexes three other worlds and successfully tells the Empire to mind its own business because of its distance from Trantor. When Terminus asks for Empirial protection, the diplomat that is sent out is a fop, knows nothing about the situation, and seems to care for nothing outside Trantor; he does, however, have the talent of seeming to promise a great deal while actually promising nothing, but this is hardly the mark of a vigorous government. By the time of "The Mule," about 300 years after Seldon, the Empire has shrunk to a few poor worlds nearest Trantor; thus is the fall of the Empire charted.

Parallel to this fall of the Empire is the rise of the First Foundation, and the changes that take place as the situations it faces change. Although the Foundation has been on Terminus for about fifty years at the time, the first Seldon crisis, the attempted annexation by Anacreon marks the beginning of the Foundation's rise to influence (power is not quite the right word, for they seem to let things go their own course as long as Terminus itself is not threatened). It also marks the passing of the rather passive governance by the scientists of the Foundation itself into the hands of the Mayors of Terminus City, a post which grows in power and significance as the population grows. The situation is quite simple: Anacreon wishes to take over Terminus, while Terminus feels that it must remain independent; there is no question of waging war to remain independent, for the resources to build weapons are not available (probably one of Seldon's reasons for selecting Terminus for the Foundation) and because the Foundationeers are philosophically against such a course. The Empire will provide no assistance whatsoever, and the scientists cannot be convinced that some decisive action must be taken to forestall the invasion. When they do not, the Mayor takes it upon himself to do so, and thus assumes political power on the planet. The strategy is quite simple: seem to give in and to supply the Kingdom of Anacreon with atomic devices, but insist that a "priesthood" which can service these devices are also a necessary part of the deal, as is the absence of an occupational force. Thus, Anacreon seems to get what it wants, Terminus retains at least a great deal of independence, and a base is established from which to disrupt any further plans Anacreon might have against Terminus.

The importance of the atomic devices and the priesthood is very clearly seen in "The Mayors," where it is effectively used to stop an invasion of Terminus and to consolidate further the influence of the Foundation. By the time of "The Traders," somewhat over fifty years later, we see that this same method of introducing atomics and the priesthood has been used on a great many worlds; the traders have gained a great deal of power by this time, and in this story the first chink is made in the usual method of expanding influence, for Ponyets does not involve the priesthood with the atomics. This device, and the rationale behind it, are fully exploited in the following story, "The Merchant Princes." Hober Mallow establishes the simple existence of trade as a means of control as effective, but less obnoxious, as the priesthood; he points out that trade and good will are necessary to anyone who has bought atomics from members of the Foundation, for the power runs out and repairs are needed—and the Foundation has the only people who can remedy those problems. In the process, he confronts the office of the Mayor, but especially the Mayor's secretary, and wins; although the name of the office remains the same, the nature of its power has shifted, for Mallow is the first of a plutocracy of businessmen who hold the office. That the mayor does not appear in the story and that his secretary has such great power suggests both that the office has degenerated and that the problems of governing, or coordinating, the ever-growing sphere of influence has gone beyond the directly democratic stage; it might be noted, however, that just as those most capable of dealing with the situation facing the Foundation in Anacreon's attempted annexation took power at that time, so also do those most capable of dealing with this situation take the power.

By the time of "The Mule," the office of Mayor has become hereditary and held by a man who is far more concerned with the forms of the office than with any real functionality. There is the possibility that had a stronger figure held the office, the Mule might have been stopped; the probabilities, though, are that he could not have been stopped by anything less than someone with equal abilities. From the point where the Mule enters the scene, the Foundation moves downhill as a political influence, only partly because of the weakness of the office of the Mayor and the man holding it. Much more important is the fact that the Mule is a mutant who has the ability to create moods and to control minds; he is totally outside the scope of the Seldon Plan. Two things that center about the Mule are enough to shatter the confidence of the members of the Foundation: first, the fact that he conquers them and the ease with which he does it, and second, the realization that this is something that was not a part of the Seldon Plan or involved in the calculations. It is obvious, too, that under the Mule the direction taken by the galaxy will not be in accord with the Seldon plan; even though galactic unification may be accomplished in much less time, the cause of civilization will be driven back. Under these circumstances, it becomes apparent that the Second Foundation must take steps to neutralize the influence of the Mule, to restore confidence in the First Foundation, and to move the course of history back to a path in closer accord with Seldon's vision. The implications are two-fold: the First Foundation will again begin to expand its sphere of trade and influence, and the Second Foundation will unobtrusively keep a careful watch and manipulate events whenever necessary.

Although much has been said about the nature of the foundations, a few words should be said explicitly about the major assumption that gives impetus to the trilogy. Because the idea of psychohistory is a prediction of a development that may happen in the far future but is not actually available to us now, Asimov had two basic choices to make in order to use the idea; he could either provide a minimum of information that would suggest the possibilities to the reader or go into great detail and, in effect, create the field himself, with the first being both the easier and the wiser course. Thus, there is not a great deal of direct information about psychohistory; in fact, most of the information is contained in the "excerpt" from the *Encyclopedia Galactica* just before the fourth section of "The Psychohistorians." One of the first requirements of this field is a sufficiently large number of humans; Seldon points out that there are approximately a quintillion people in the galaxy governed by the Empire. He seems to suggest that something less than that might be sufficient, but it is also significant that psychohistory only became a precise science during the lifetime of Hari Seldon; before that it was only a vague set of axioms. It also seems to be true of psychohistory that, while it evolves from the individual to the larger mass, it can work from the larger mass down to, at least, significant individuals or individuals who play roles at significant moments, although the accuracy of its predictions on this level is much less than its accuracy on the large scale. Another necessary element in psychohistory seems to be an extensive and detailed knowledge of the past, both in its trends and in its particular events; at his trial, Hari Seldon makes the claim that he has more complete knowledge of the history of the Empire than any man in the audience or among the judges. It is interesting to note in this connection that Asimov has constructed a fill-in-the-blank outline of history that can be filled in so that it portrays three distinct historical eras in three different countries; on one level, this is something that any psychohistorian should be able to do, but he would also have to know the particulars of each situation, the ways in which they differ, and the relations between stimuli and action in these cases. Another major element of psychohistory is mathematical sophistication, for the predictions and the degree of probability of each is derived mathematically. The precise nature of the mathematical, statistical processes that are used are never explained, but they do seem to have some similarity to symbolic logic and to the mathematics used in dealing with the uncertainty principle. The final element involved in any valid psychohistory is that the masses of people who are the basis for the mathematical calculations must be unaware of psychohistory, for if they are not, their actions will not have the randomness that is required; at most, a small group can be aware and working toward a change.

Because of these elements and because psychohistory not only predicts future events and trends but also moments at which the trends of history might be successfully altered, we can see the urgency that Seldon feels in forcing the government to establish the First Foundation—that is, even though five hundred years might pass before the Empire finally dissolves, it is necessary to introduce the machinery through which the 30,000 years of dark ages might be reduced to 1,000 years so that it will be firmly entrenched when the fall finally comes. Even though the compendium of all knowledge that is the announced purpose of the Foundation on Terminus is a ploy, something that the government in power can accept, the purpose of the foundation is nevertheless to preserve knowledge and to advance it, concentrated in one place so that it will not be lost and so that its influence can spread when necessary. Furthermore, by making public this First Foundation and its avowed purpose, the Second Foundation is hidden from sight and can be allowed to develop without public knowledge and without interference; they, too, are absolutely necessary to the plan to shorten the interregnum to a thousand years, but since they are the psychohistorians, it is essential that their existence be kept secret. From these elements, then, arise the stories and the sweep of the whole that constitutes the Foundation trilogy.

The themes of the individual stories all tend to revolve around these larger themes that hold the trilogy together. For example, in "The Psychohistorians," much of the thematic material is centered around the nature of the field, the way in which Seldon forces events, and the methods which a decaying Empire uses to preserve the status quo, treating each of these in some depth. In addition, Asimov does a fine job in this story of giving a sense of a young man's first visit to the planet-wide capitol city of the galaxy; it is not so much a matter that he goes into great detail about any part of this description, but rather that he focuses on the telling incidents, such as Gaal Dornick's disappointment at not seeing Trantor from space and his elevator ride to the observation deck: a great deal of information both about Gaal and about the Empire centered in Trantor are packed into these rather brief scenes. In fact, this is a technique that Asimov uses extremely effectively throughout the trilogy; he focuses attention on a few scenes and a few key individuals and chooses details with which he fills out these scenes, and thus the reader comes to feel that he has seen much more of the situation than he has in a direct way. For example, when Gaal goes up the elevator, we learn that it travels at such speed that foot grips are necessary, suggesting a great deal of the technology available on Trantor as opposed to other places in the galaxy; we learn that most of Trantor is underground, with the building which Dornick is in rising only five hundred feet; we learn that most Trantorians rarely go places where they can see the sky, which may be symbolic also of the way the government is run; we learn something of the awe and admiration which much of the population seems to feel toward Trantor, both in itself and as a symbol of the Empire; we learn something about Gaal Dornick, as well as a number of other details. A great deal is packed into a rather brief, two-page scene.

The two stories which follow this one, "The Encyclopedists" and "The Mayors," also embody similar techniques, dealing with the first and second crises faced by the First Foundation. In the fifty years that pass between the founding of Terminus as the Foundation planet and that first crisis, a great deal must have happened; after all, approximately 100,000 people have been moved from Trantor to Terminus, they have established themselves on a rather difficult planet, a city has sprung up, conflicts have risen between the scientists and the people necessary to support them, the work on the Encyclopedia has gone on, four of the neighboring planets have broken away from Empirial rule—and these are only some of the major happenings. However, for the purposes of the overall history of the two foundations, these are important only as background, so Asimov only hints at them, slipping in a detail here and a detail there that allows the reader to fill in a good deal of the background. Just as individuals are relatively unimportant to psychohistory, so, too, are most events unimportant except as they indicate trends and possible directions; much more important than individuals and most events are those situations and events which the trends can change, when history can evolve in several directions. For example, if Terminus capitulated to Anacreon, it is probable that the interregnum between civilizations would last the original 30,000 years, for the First Foundation would have been firmly controlled by someone with no such mission as they have and would have no chance to build their sphere of influence. Very much the same is true of "The Mayors"; much has happened in the meantime, with changes taking place in the society and in the relations between Terminus and Anacreon; for that matter, the solution reached in "The Encyclopedists" is never explained there, but rather is shown in "The Mayors" through the action. Thus, each of these stories deals with a situation in which the direction of history can be changed, and each story focuses very carefully on a rather restricted set of events. However, the events focused on are crucial ones, ones showing both the crisis and its effects; by the astute use of details, Asimov manages to make these scenes come alive and to provide enough information about what has happened since the previous story so that we feel that we have actually been following a history and are involved in its flow. Without the successful application of this technique, the Foundation trilogy could have fallen far short of its goal.

A very similar technique is used in his creation of characters to people the crises and adventures. There are a number of memorable characters in these stories: Salvor Hardin, Jorane Sutt, Hober Mallow, General Bel Riose, the Mule, Bayta Darell, Han Pritcher, Arkady Darell, and Preem Palver suggest themselves immediately, but others also stand out against the background quite clearly. As we read these stories, we have a feeling that we know these characters quite well. However, on very close analysis, we can see that they are not all that well-developed, that only a very few characteristics have been given to each of them, and that they are really quite flat. This is not to suggest that Asimov should have done a better job at characterization, but rather to congratulate him for choosing those details of characterization so carefully and making them fit the character in a particular situation so well that we feel that they are real and solid. Part of this success is due to the fact that much of the characterization is done through the action in which the characters participate—that is, we watch them do things in a particular way and then imagine what kind of person would do that sort of thing in that way, thus drawing on our experiences with people to flesh out the skeleton that Asimov has provided. In this way, a number of things can be accomplished: the reader can feel that he knows the characters, Asimov can spend a minimum of time on individuals, and, thus, he can spend a maximum of time on the subject at hand, the historical processes of a civilization.

Reading the Foundation trilogy is an exceptional experience in many ways. It has the sweep of the "Space Opera," and the details of a closely examined situation on a small scale. Its major interest is in societies· and in historical processes, but we also seem to know the characters well. Very few works of any kind, but especially very few pieces of science fiction, work well on both the general and the specific levels at the same time; that Asimov did so in the early 1950s, before science fiction had gained even such sophistication as it now has, makes this all the more impressive.

THE DEMOLISHED MAN

Alfred Bester

Hugo Award, 1952

The Demolished Man is a science fiction detective
novel. Its story-line is slightly modified to meet
the demands of the science fiction elements, but it is
easily recognizable as the process of investigation of a
murder and the subsequent gathering of clues that will
bring the guilty to justice. However, this particular
murder takes place in a future society in which sev-
enty years have passed since a serious crime of this
nature has occurred, largely because there is a fairly
good-sized population of telepaths scattered throughout the professions; a part of their training and their
oath requires that they report any evidence of contemplated crimes before they occur. Thus, in addition to the detective interest, there is an examination
of the advantages and drawbacks of being telepathic
in a predominantly "normal" society.

There is a variety of mystery story which lets the
reader know early in the story who the murderer is
and then allows him to watch the inevitable gathering of clues until the guilty person is captured. Of
necessity, this is one of that kind of mystery story;
with the presence of highly skilled telepaths, the person who committed the crime is known within an
hour after the investigation begins. The interesting
questions, then, that take the place of the suspense of
the straight detective novel are: how, in this kind of
society, does one go about planning and carrying out

a murder without being detected beforehand, and how does the telepathic Prefect of Police convict a man he knows to be guilty if it is required that all evidence used to convict a man be objective and if the testimony of a telepath is not admissible evidence in a court of law? These two points determine the direction and the nature of the mystery-story aspect of the novel and they also set the background for the other areas that Bester explores in this novel.

Ben Reich is the murderer. He is the absolute head of Monarch Utilities and Resources, Inc., one of the most powerful firms in the solar system. His victim is Craye D'Courtney, head of The D'Courtney Cartel, Monarch's rival. The struggle between the two companies serves as the surface motivation of the murder, for Ben Reich begins to plan as soon as he offers a merger with equal partnership to D'Courtney and receives a reply which he interprets as being a refusal. Thus even this early in the novel, the reader is given a clue that there is something more behind the murder, something that even Reich is not consciously aware of, for the code used is given to the reader and he can see that the message accepts Reich's offer rather than rejects it. It is, however, much later in the novel that this element is explained—to the reader, to Ben Reich, and to the police.

Once Reich has decided that he must commit murder, the way that he proceeds so that he can avoid being detected before the act, and hopefully afterward, is extremely complex and extremely clever, as one might expect from a man who has managed to hold and expand a company like Monarch; it helps, too, having the advantages of that position, money and power. His first step is to find a 1st Class Esper who will accept sufficient bribery and break the rigidly imposed Esper Oath and, also, one who can be dominated in spite of his talent. There are several reasons for this. First, Reich can gain necessary information through the Esper's talents that can be gained in no other way; in this case, Reich must know when D'Courtney will be in New York and exactly where he will be when there, both of which are highly guarded secrets. Second, a 1st Class Esper can help a great deal to mask Reich's thought patterns and help Reich know when he must be particularly careful about what thoughts he is revealing when other Espers are about. Third, especially because the Esper Oath has never been seriously broken, a 1st Class Esper has access to circles in which he can find out exactly what measures the police are taking in their investigation. The Esper in this case is Augustus Tate, E.M.D. I; he is open to bribery because the Esper Guild takes 95% of his income to train new Espers and to bring the benefits eventually to the entire world, programs which Tate very much resents. Once he knows where D'Courtney will be staying (in the Orchid Room of the home of Maria Beaumont) and how he will be guarded, his next step is to find a book of games that he had noted five years earlier, carefully deface all but the one game that will allow him to find and murder D'Courtney (remember, no one is supposed to know he is there), have it appraised to see if the experts can tell he has mutilated it, and send it to Maria Beaumont, hoping that she will use it during the party that D'Courtney will attend. Furthermore, because Tate knows the location of the book, he can act in such a way that it will appear that he just happened to find it; the appraisal of a gift before giving it is one of the social customs of the period, so that will raise few questions. His third step is to visit Monarch's research facilities, ostensibly to check on progress, but in reality to steal a visual knock-out capsule which blinds the victim and abolishes his sense of space and time temporarily; this is to be used on the guards at the entrance of the Orchid Suite. Fourth, he will visit Psych-Songs, Inc. to get an anti-gambling jingle for the Recreation Department at Monarch, which has been established as a legitimate request earlier; at the same time, he asks the song writer what the catchiest, most persistent tune she ever wrote was. Again, this seems perfectly natural, but Reich wants the tune as a block against all but the deepest Esper probes. Finally, he finds his weapon, an antique (twentieth-century) knife-pistol, at a pawn shop run by an ex-Esper 2 who was ruined by a previous association with Reich. He makes sure that the bullets are removed so that the murder weapon will be even harder to identify. After all this preparation, all that is left is for him to go to Maria's party and hope that she takes the bait he has sent her so that he can carry out his plan.

Everything goes as expected, until the moment that Reich faces D'Courtney; then things begin to fall apart. First, he talks to D'Courtney, who insists that he accepted Reich's offer instead of refusing it. Reich becomes almost hysterical, refusing to believe this and intent on killing him. (It is interesting to note that D'Courtney is dying anyway, which Reich knows, but he feels frustrated at the thought of not being able to kill him.) The second thing that goes wrong is that D'Courtney's daughter, whom Reich had no knowledge of, bursts into the room just before the murder, and then runs out of the house before Reich can react; there is now a witness to the murder. Finally, before Reich can leave the house as he had planned, blood drips from his shirt, which leads to the discovery of the murder (he is not particularly suspected, since the game was a search for others in the dark). The police are called in, led by Lincoln Powell Ph.D.1, Prefect of the Psychotic Division. Perhaps the most accomplished Esper in the society, he is an excellent match for Reich. Almost as soon as he encounters the group he suspects Reich, and very shortly he has the opportunity to confirm this with a cleverly set-up glimpse into his mind (this involves getting past the guard of both Tate and the Esper-lawyer whom Reich has brought in, as well as the mental blocks that Reich has arranged).

From this point on, we are concerned with Powell's solving of the case. Most of the action traces the means by which Powell uncovers, step by step, the plans that Reich made, the apparent reasons for them, and the materials which will support the case. His tracks have been quite well hidden, his use of a 1st Class Esper helps him to discover where the police are looking and to arrange diversions, and he uses his wealth to make sure that key people are hard to find, in natural-seeming ways, when the police wish to talk with them. As one might expect of a master-detective, Powell is gradually able to accumulate the evidence that he needs to make his case. It is, however, a confrontation of two extremely able men who, moreover, like and respect each other. We expect that the detective will gain the clues that he needs, and consequently Bester is able to concentrate more attention during this gathering of clues on other matters than the specific case at hand.

It might be possible to label most of these other interests as psychological. That is, many of them are related in one way or another to studying the way that man's mind works in certain situations. One example, the central matter concerns the fact that not only do we watch the plans that Ben Reich makes as they move toward murder, but we also know a good deal of his psychology while he is making these plans. Furthermore, at least an element of Lincoln Powell's investigation of this crime is an attempt to understand *why* Reich did it. This becomes particularly important after he discovers that D'Courtney accepted the offer of merger and that he cannot prove an economic motive for the crime.

The novel opens with Reich waking from a dream of The Man With No Face, screaming. His resident analyst, a 2nd Class Esper who cannot reach the deeper levels of Reich's mind, suggests that this apparition in his dreams is D'Courtney. However, the dreams continue even after he has killed D'Courtney and in much the same way. Some of the explanation of this is suggested when Lincoln Powell sees in Barbara D'Courtney's mind an image of herself and Ben Reich linked as Siamese twins. It concludes when Powell uses the Mass Cathexis Measure (one Esper tapping the pool of latent psychic energy contributed by all other Espers) in order to force Reich to face the truth—that is, The Man With No Face is a composite of himself and Craye D'Courtney, Craye being Reich's father.

As the Mosaic Multiplex Prosecution Computer of the District Attorney's office indicated (a fact which was not understood at that time), the crime was a crime of passion rather than a crime with an economic motive, a crime to punish a father whom Reich felt had rejected and abandoned him. Even so, until Powell is able to force him to face the image squarely, Reich is unwilling and unable to admit to himself that

78

he has any motive other than economics or that he recognizes D'Courtney as his father. In addition, Reich also demonstrates guilt feelings, which he does not admit to himself, and, after the case has been officially closed because there is no economic motive nor a motive of passion which can be objectively proven, Reich shows an inner desire for punishment by unconsciously planting a series of boobytraps for himself, which he narrowly escapes. This possibility was suggested earlier, when Reich spoke of being committed to Demolition. In retrospect, it almost seems as though he planned, ultimately, to be caught and punished.

Demolition is another interesting psychological element in this novel. Instead of executing criminals of various sorts, particularly those who operate on a large scale, a process is used to destroy certain memories and mental patterns that have been developed since birth. When this process is complete, the Demolished Man is ready for rebirth, a new beginning. He has not lost the powers of his mind nor the potentialities that he had before Demolition, however, only, the memories and patterns are gone that made him a destructive rather than a constructive force. It is not an easy process, either in terms of the patient or of time. The patient is conscious of what is happening to him, but powerless to stop it. Ben Reich's Demolition will take slightly over a year before he reaches rebirth, and his metamorphosis is quicker than most. This process does not render any human life useless or a burden on the rest of the society; instead, it recognizes that, especially in a society such as the one in which Powell and Reich live, anyone who has the courage and the ability to rebel against society is one who has basic abilities that should be preserved but converted into a positive force for society's benefit. Ben Reich, as we have seen him throughout the novel, with enormous strengths and energies as well as with weaknesses, is a perfect example of this theory.

There is also a love interest in this novel, although it takes an unusual twist because it, too, is a part of the psychological exploration in the novel. On one level, the purely physical level, there are the girls who would dearly love to get Ben Reich into bed with them, several of them successfully scheming to do so. This, however, is minor, and both the schemes and the results are barely mentioned. Maria Beaumont is another minor example of the attitudes of the society; she is commonly known as the Gilt Corpse because of the "cosmetic" surgery, etc., to make her body more attractive, and her parties, including the one at which D'Courtney is killed, are known for their semi-sexual games. Again, this is suggested rather than detailed.

Interestingly, the major love interest involves Lincoln Powell. The Esper Guild requires its members to marry another Esper by the time they are forty; Powell is rapidly approaching that age. He is also somewhat romantic and idealistic, which means that he is not willing simply to find someone who will fulfill the Guild requirement; love must play a part. This makes his relationship with Mary Noyes assume importance. Mary is an Esper-2, which allows them to converse on a telepathic level, reasonably deeply, and she is desperately in love with Powell. This fact, and the fact that he is not in love with her, are open secrets between them; nevertheless, she hopes that he won't find someone else before he must get married. Once he finds Barbara D'Courtney, however, a triangle develops, although it is not the traditional sort of triangle. Powell falls in love with her immediately. We discover this through Mary Noyes, for Powell won't admit even that he is in love with Barbara until the end of the novel. The thing which complicates this love story and ties it to the psychological theme of the novel is the fact that Barbara has suffered traumatic shock from seeing her father killed by her brother. Through the psychiatric techniques of the society of Espers, her conscious mind returns to babyhood, although her sub-conscious mind retains all its memories and patterns; the process of moving back to the mental equivalent of her chronological age takes only a short time. Because of this, however, we see her affection for Powell grow—first, there is admiration for a father-figure, then an adolescent passion, and, finally, adult love, during which she senses the violence of love and hate in her subconsciousness. At the same time, Powell uses her memories to try to find out as much about the murder as possible, a rationalization to keep her at his house. Furthermore, Mary Noyes is Barbara's babysitter, and it is to her credit that she is able to accept what is happening, knowing that Powell loves Barbara, not her, and that Barbara is falling in love with Powell. It is, however, a shock when she discovers that Barbara is a latent telepath—thus that she and Powell can marry, meeting the requirements of the Guild.

In addition to the love and crime interests involved here, Bester uses these relationships to suggest something of the nature of the subconscious mind. The web of associations is so dense and so cross-wired that one could easily be lost, unable to find the path back to the surface; even Powell, as good and experienced as he is at this, is lost for three hours at one point in his investigation.

Finally, there is the exploration of the telepathic phenomena and its workings. One of the assumptions made, which makes this novel different from many other novels exploring this topic, is that the relationship between Espers and Normals is cordial, with very little envy or discord between them. Furthermore, Bester does not explain how telepathy arose in the society, nor how many of them there are. However, in addition to the uses of telepathy in psychological work and in crime-solving, he does consider other facets of this phenomenon. For example, he gives some suggestions about telepathic conversation on two levels. With individuals, he suggests that images are involved, rather than only words, though he is limited by the fact that he must use words to describe this. In groups, the patterns woven in multiple conversations are also interesting; here he uses typographical tricks to give an impression of what might be done. As in any other group of varying ability, there is something of a caste system, although the best of the Espers ignore this, as much as possible. Perhaps one of the most fascinating facts about the Esper Guild, to which almost every Esper belongs, is its interest in finding talented individuals, in researching the causes of the talent, and in trying to generate this talent within the general population. Most members are quite willing to pay the high dues (up to 95% of their income) or to spend a great deal of volunteer time at these pursuits in order to find, develop, and stimulate telepathy in others. They also have a very rigidly enforced code of ethics, committing them as a group to working for the good of mankind. The anguish of the telepath who has broken this code and been cast out of their fellowship gives an indication of the force which compels adherence. Thus, in addition to the background necessary to the story of a telepathic detective, the reader is given some additional facets of what might be entailed by the existence of a number of telepaths in a society.

Bester does not go into a great deal of detail on any of the points mentioned, often suggesting rather than exploring in depth. And there are other facets of this society that are suggested in even less detail, such as the fact that a trip between Earth and Venus seems as easy and as swift as a trip today between two cities in the United States. It should be remembered, however, that this is, primarily, a detective story, but that Bester could provide so many details about facets of society while also writing an excellent mystery story is to his credit.

CHILDHOOD'S END

Arthur C. Clarke

1953

Childhood's End is a novel of sweeping vision that nevertheless manages to bring to the sweep and the vision a sense of detailed reality. In many ways similar to *2001: A Space Odyssey*, this is a better novel, although it would probably not make as visually interesting a motion picture. Whereas *2001* is rather suggestive and vague, *Childhood's End* is more concrete, detailed, and complex. Perhaps its major difficulty lies in the necessary telling of the story from the point-of-view of a detached omniscient observer with a large number of summarizing passages and only a few passages which focus on specific characters; in addition, the action of this novel takes place over approximately 150 years, which makes it almost impossible to use a single human individual as an emotional focus. But while this approach has some weaknesses in holding a reader's interest through identification with a particular character, it does focus on four individuals in different eras and it also allows the reader to see the entire process of mankind's apotheosis from a number of vantage points and realize many facets of this process that would not be known to a single human being. Although there are a number of human and non-human individuals with whom the reader can sympathize and even identify, the interest in the novel lies primarily in the vision of what the next step beyond man might be and the process of reaching that point of fulfillment.

The novel is divided into three major sections: "Earth and the Overlords," "The Golden Age," and "The Last Generation." Through these sections, two basic topics are examined in rather full detail: man's contact with an apparently superior alien race and the future development of mankind. At first glance, and stated in this way, these topics may seem unrelated, even as they are developed in the book, with about the first two-thirds devoted to the first contact idea and the last one-third examining mankind's apotheosis. Despite the apparent dichotomy of interest, however, these two areas of interest are closely entwined, for the first lays the groundwork for the second, creating the situation in which the apotheosis can occur. This interweaving of theme is accomplished through three related stories of people who were "firsts." In the initial section, the focus is on Rikki Stormgren, Secretary-General of the United Nations at the time the Overlords appear and the first man to have contact with them. In the second and third sections, the stories of George and Jean Greggson, the parents of the children who make the initial breakthrough toward the new being, and of Jan Rodericks, the first and only man to reach the stars, are intertwined. Through this rather complicated structural setup, a variety of aspects of the major thematic points are examined and brought into focus.

The story of Stormgren is the story of the first contact with the Overlords and its effects on mankind. The aliens appear suddenly—just as mankind is within days of sending spaceships to the moon. Their huge ships appear over every major city on Earth, as well as over the American and Russian rocket bases; the size of the ships, the number, and the sudden appearance have an immediate and profound psychological effect on the people of Earth. This effect is sharpened by the flawless English of the leader and the brilliance of the talk that is broadcast over all channels on Earth. One should also note the swiftness and the means by which the dictates of the Overlords are enforced. The major reaction produced is awe at the overwhelming intellectual and technological superiority of these aliens. For the most part, however, life on Earth continues as before, for these aliens, to whom men give the name Overlords, remain largely aloof and make very few demands. Possibly the two most important things that they impose on Earth is the cessation of war and the formation of a single world government. Here, consider that these demands are accepted with very little resistance, for most men either see the wisdom of these actions or welcome the fact that they are no longer responsible for such decisions. Only a small portion resists, approximately 7% of the total population of Earth. The story-line in this section involves Secretary-General Stormgren's attempts to implement the policies of the Overlords, with which he is largely in agreement, and to placate the members of the resistance movements. There is little action in this section; a good deal of Stormgren's time is spent in conference with Karellen, the Supervisor of Earth, with his assistant Pieter Van Ryberg, and with Alexander Wainright, leader of the Freedom League. Even when he is kidnapped by the radical wing of the Freedom League, it is his conversations with his captors that we witness. In short, action is not particularly important to advancing the theme or the human reaction in this section, and action for its own sake would only be an obstacle. Thus, such action as there is focuses attention on two major groups: those who intelligently and knowingly accept the conditions of the Overlords and try to implement them (Stormgren and Van Ryberg) and those who resist (Wainright and the kidnappers). The resistance movement, whether it be the moderate wing led by Wainright or the radical wing, is motivated by the belief that humans should work out their own destiny.

Despite the fact that the interest is focused on two groups which oppose each other, the case for the benevolence of the Overlords is furthered by their interaction. Thus, when both Wainright and Stormgren agree that for the first time in human history no man need go hungry or that the idea of a strong World Federation is, in principle, desirable (even though they disagree on the means of achieving these), it is a convincing case for the rightness of what the Overlords do. Or when Stormgren's kidnappers seem willing to accept the Overlords' absolute ban on cruelty to animals, it is difficult for the reader to do otherwise. The other major focus achieved by Stormgren's round of conferences is on Karellen, the Earth Supervisor. Through him, we receive some suggestion of what the Overlords are like and what they are about; his relationship with Stormgren leaves a very favorable impression. In addition to these direct sources of information, we also have the commentary of the omniscient narrator, who summarizes worldwide events and who points out factors which are not accessible through the characters. Through this narrator, two things are stressed: first, because of the presence and intervention of the Overlords, directly and indirectly (by halting war, more resources are made generally available for example), the standard of living for all of mankind began rising steadily; second, despite the beneficial effects, this presence had an inhibiting effect on the creative activities of mankind in both the arts and the sciences.

While the first section is mainly concerned with outlining the first contact between man and alien beings and with the effects of that contact, the second section, which returns us to the situation fifty years later, is concerned with more solidly establishing the trends suggested in the first section and laying the groundwork for the events of the third. It is a transitional section, the emphasis being almost entirely on the human element. Through the commentary of the omniscient observer, we are given an overview of a united world in which the former names of countries are merely conveniences for the postal system. Ignorance, war, poverty, fear, crime and disease have been almost totally eradicated. The necessities of life are provided for all, so that one need not work or may work at something he enjoys for whatever luxuries he wants. The higher standard of education has provided men with the resources to handle the greatly increased amount of leisure time. Travel is fast and free. Life is much more tranquil and leisurely. In many ways, life has become more gracious than at any time in the past. On the other hand, life is not as exciting as it once was; with the elimination of strife and conflict, the creative arts declined, although the old musical works are performed more than ever. Additionally, the presence of the vastly superior science and technology of the Overlords has replaced fundamental scientific research. Except for a very small minority, however, these things are not really missed.

Against this general situation, we are introduced to George and Jean Greggson and to Jan Rodericks at a party given by Rupert Boyce in honor of his new house and his new wife. Also among the guests at this party is one of the Overlords, Rashaverak, who has been attracted by Boyce's extensive library on paraphysics—magic, telepathy, divining, and psychic research. The party itself and the things that happen while the party is going on seem to be designed mainly to give some idea of what life is like at this time. After the party is over, Boyce and his wife, the Greggsons (they are not married yet), Jan Rodericks and another man experiment with a type of Ouija board for Rashaverak, who is an observer. This builds to the point at which Jan Rodericks, who is one of the few who are still space-smitten, asks which star is the Overlords' sun, something unknown to humans and a carefully guarded secret. However, the Ouija board spells it out, as a number from the star catalogues; immediately after that, Jean faints. The suggestion is that it was through Jean that the answer was transmitted. The Overlords are extremely interested in Jan, who asked the question, and Jean, who answered it. Of the two, however, it is Jean who excites them most; they consider her the most important human alive. She is not what they are looking for, but she is in contact with their goal, the implication being that it will be her children that hold what they are seeking. The only other suggestion given at this point is that some sort of psychic phenomena is involved.

Except for a short passage in which George definitely decides that Jean is the girl he wants to marry, and Jean expresses fear of the Overlords and their purposes, the rest of this section of the novel is devoted to how Jan Rodericks makes use of the knowledge he has rather surprisingly gained. Although it is presented in some detail, which is necessary to make it believable and provides the opportunity to add some other facets of life on Earth under the Overlords, the outline of what Rodericks does is quite simple. He first checks the number against the star catalogues at the Royal Astronomical Society and compares the information with what many men have observed about the course taken by the Overlords' supply ships. Then, quite accidentally, in the course of a conversation with his brother-in-law, he learns of the Overlords' interest in animal specimens and that they have requested one of a whale and a giant squid in combat. He seeks out the man who will provide this, aligns himself with this project, and creates a hideaway inside the whale, complete with oxygen and other such provisions as he will need during the journey. It is interesting to note that all his calculations are based on Einstein's relativity theory, including the fact he will age only a few months even though the round trip may take approximately 80 years, Earth time. This section of the novel ends with Karellen's announcing that Jan has stowed away and explaining that man, in his present stage of evolution, cannot hope to be able to cope with the immensity of space, much less the overwhelming powers and forces that exist out there. Privately, he also reflects that this is as much of the truth as he can give.

The last section of the novel returns initially to George and Jean, who are now married and have two children. George, a set designer for television, is upset with the state of the arts. This leads him to consider the colony of New Athens, set on two linked islands, whose purpose is to regain something of mankind's former independence and to create conditions where human creativity in the arts and sciences can once again develop and flourish through applied social engineering. For about fifteen pages, we are given a brief history of the colony and a view of the Greggsons as they settle into life there, both through the omniscient narrator and through focus on the Greggsons. Not only do we learn about the island, but also about life in most other places in the world, as they react to what they find there. For example, Jean reacts negatively to the fact that there is a kitchen in their home, whereas one in other places would be able to dial a central facility for food in five minutes. Only after this is firmly established do the final actions begin. A *tsunami* hits the islands while Jeff, their son, is exploring the uninhabited island; he is saved twice, once when an inner voice tells him to run and once when a large boulder blocking his path is destroyed. In these actions, and in the reported conversations among the Overlords, it is apparent that Jeff Greggson is somehow the key to what they expect to happen; his parents are bewildered and frightened. About six weeks later, Jeff begins to dream of strange worlds, a fact which interests the Overlords a great deal. Through exchanges between Karellen and Rashaverak, we are told that the places he dreams of are actual locations in the universe, although his last dream is of a place beyond the experience of the Overlords. Shortly after that, Jennifer Anne Greggson closes her eyes permanently, since she has no further need of them, and lies there contentedly rattling her rattle—which is half a meter away from her.

The Overlords now feel free to explain many things about what is happening and what their role has been. For example, they reveal that they are merely agents of powers as far beyond them as they are beyond man, that all they have been doing was designed to create the conditions for what they call Total Breakthrough, and that they are a race which can never make this breakthrough, although they continue to hope and to study it to see if they can discover what might happen. The Greggson children become more and more removed from Earthly life, more and more in contact with something else. Furthermore, almost all children below the age of ten join them very rapidly. Finally, the Overlords remove them all to a continent of their own, to give them room to do what they must do, to protect other human lives, and to observe them. Before they do this, however, Karellen explains what has happened and why; in addition to the points mentioned above, he suggests that had these powers developed on their own in the kind of cultural environment that was developing when the Overlords came and without guidance of any kind, that would have resulted in a cancerous growth of great danger in the universe. Consequently, development at all cultural levels had to be disrupted in order for this new condition to grow and develop properly. Thus, mankind as we know it now is finished, but it has provided the seed for something much greater. Once this message is understood, nearly all of mankind decides that quick, instant death is preferable to lingering slowly without any hope of a future.

It is at this point that the story of Jan Rodericks becomes important once again. In fact, it is almost as though the Overlords knew his plan from the beginning and allowed him to go through with it, serving both their goals and his. For the reader, Jan's visit to the world of the Overlords serves to provide further information about them and to show the differences between man and Overlord. Although it is brief, an interesting portrait of a city built by a flying race whose eyes see in a different spectrum of light is presented; for example, there are graceful buildings with doors opening into the air and a city with few, if any, streets. Thematically, this visit serves to further the idea that mankind was not meant to go to the stars, for Jan Rodericks barely retains his sanity in the face of what he sees, and he is being carefully guided by the Overlords so that he will not confront anything that is truly dangerous to him.

When he returns to Earth, Rodericks is the only man left alive. Karellen shows him the progress of the children, all of whom are practically motionless in a pattern that covers an entire continent, though mentally they are apparently quite active, for at one point they destroy all animal and vegetable life around them. They have also changed the courses of rivers and tested their powers in other ways; Karellen believes that the Overmind is training them and that they are still coming together and developing. When the moon begins to spin on its axis, the moment of apotheosis is near; the Overlords invite Jan to come with them, but he chooses to remain, as they hoped he would. He is thus able to describe for them, and for the reader, the moment of apotheosis. A great misty network of light spreads over the globe from a burning column of fire, spreading outwards as it moves away from Earth. The landscape is brightly lit in a fantastic variety of colors. Then gradually the atmosphere begins to leave and cataclysmic shocks shake the Earth, until the core gives up its hoarded substance to nourish the new being. At the end, Karellen mourns for his race, for they cannot lose their individual souls in order to become a part of a larger soul.

There are several minor but interesting points made through the book. One of these is the suggestion that time is not linear but, instead, that all time exists at any given point; this is why, for example, Jean is able to provide an answer to Jan's question, since she is in contact with her son who would know that information; also, this explains why the Overlords must carefully prepare mankind for their (the Overlords') physical appearance. Minds early in history had seen the role of the Overlords in mankind's end and thus used the image of the Devil for the Overlords. There are also some suggestions about the nature and use of power; a very small amount applied at the right time and the right way will achieve much more than the massive doses that mankind tends to use. There are suggestions of ways in which our resources could be used to improve life on Earth, as well as warnings about what too much comfort might do to man's creative spirit. And there are many more such ideas touched on in the course of the novel. All of this is dominated, however, by what amounts to a religious vision; one way to state the theme of the novel is "Unless a man loseth his soul, he cannot gain it." This is what the children of man do as they lose their individual souls and rid themselves of their mortal bodies in order to become a part of a larger, more universal soul. In this way, the appearance of the Overlords is appropriate, for they are unable to lose their souls, to lose their individuality, or to become a part of something greater than themselves. They are creatures of intellect rather than of spirit; they thus fit the image that we mortals have of the Devil. However, there are, of course, modifications—such as their benevolence and the purpose for which they would destroy mankind. But, basically, *Childhood's End* is a religious vision of the way that mankind might develop and the desirability of that direction.

CONJURE WIFE

Fritz Leiber

1953; 8th Annual Mrs. Ann Radcliffe Award, 1st Prize

In some ways this may seem to be a rather strange book to include in a volume devoted to science fiction. The award that it has won is for Gothic Horror novels, a fact boldly announced on the cover of the paperback edition. In addition, it is set in the present, at a small, private college, and its characters seem, by and large, people you might meet anywhere, but especially on a small-college campus. Furthermore, the subject matter of this novel is witchcraft and magic, which is not one of the more prominent concerns of science fiction.

Nevertheless, *Conjure Wife*, in its *approach* to this topic, contains some of the typical qualities of science fiction; for example, it is similar to *The Incomplete Enchanter*, but because it is set in the present, in the world as we know it, it is often not considered as science fiction. Careful investigation, however, proves the reverse, and since the case for the existence and nature of magic is developed very carefully in a step-by-step fashion, this discussion will also follow that pattern.

Basically, the first chapter does two things: it establishes the major character, Norman Saylor, in and against the background, and it provides the incident that unravels all that follows. Norman is a professor of sociology at Hempnell College and has established a good professional reputation for his scholarly work dealing with female psychology and the parallels between primitive superstition and modern neuroses. He is still relatively young, something of an intellectual rebel, and a lover of many things in life that go beyond the pleasures condoned by Hempnell. Hempnell is a small, private college, very proud of its tradition and its image, and very rigid in the standards of decorum and conduct that it imposes on students and faculty alike. Norman is more than a little surprised that he and his wife, Tansy, have managed to stay there as long as they have, modifying their behavior enough to be accepted—but not so much as to compromise what they truly enjoy. Norman gives Tansy full credit for this, for fighting Hempnell on its own terms (little does he know at this point what those terms are), allowing him to carry on his research, even transforming him from a rather lazy man into a happily productive scholar. We learn most of this early in the novel when, after finishing a scholarly paper, Norman is exhilarated, and in somewhat of a devilish mood, wants to do something slightly forbidden to celebrate. On impulse, he goes through the drawers of his wife's dressing room and is aghast when he finds graveyard dirt, nail-clippings, silver filings, and other things—the paraphernalia of magic. Tansy comes home, unexpectedly, and discovers him. Thus the novel begins explosively.

In studying this novel, note first that Norman is a student of the sociological factors of primitive superstition, which includes and involves magic; in addition, he has a large fund of background knowledge to draw on when he needs it. But because he is a scholar, he has a tendency to be rational and analytical, viewing the subject of his studies and the contents of his wife's drawer as sheer superstition with no basis in reality. This attitude inhibits his acceptance of the things that happen and his capacity to act on what he knows. This skepticism of his is, of course, very helpful to the reader in moving into the story and accepting its premises. Note too that the nature of the college is such that there are strong undercurrents of faculty and individual rivalry, though things may seem placid on the surface; this both lays the groundwork for the struggle to come and alternately reinforces both of the sides of Norman's thinking on the matter. Finally, the paraphernalia of magic that Norman finds establishes the subject of the novel, as well as suggesting some of the means with which Tansy has used to defend them from Hempnell's oppressiveness and make their stay there successful and relatively pleasant. This first chapter establishes the situation, the mood, the central characters, the direction that the action of the novel will take, and the topic to be explored. After this, the reader is well-prepared to move gradually deeper into a world where magic *may* be real.

The next chapter and a half details the discussion between Tansy and Norman about her practice of magic and gives the first indications that Norman may be wrong in his rationalist's belief that magic is nothing but superstition. Of course, Tansy is extremely upset about what her husband found and reacts, at first, very emotionally. Norman, however, insists that this is something they must talk about. What we see here is Norman's rational, analytical, skeptical, and rather close-minded approach to the matter; he is not willing to consider her explanations, but instead feels that he must talk her out of all this nonsense. Because Tansy admits that she is not sure that her magic has any practical effects, he is successful in getting her not only to tell him all about it but also to burn all of her paraphernalia and the little voodoo devices she has hidden around the house. In the course of the conversation, three suggestions which will be important for the theme and their story are made. First, it is suggested that women are closer to the more basic, more ancient aspects of life and feeling than are men (this has some basis in psychological theory); second, that three other faculty wives—Evelyn Sawtelle, Hulda Gunnison, and Flora Carr—not only practice white (protective) magic but also dabble in black magic. And finally, Tansy says she began because of the things she wanted to happen, or not to happen, to someone she loves, suggesting that millions of other women have done the same thing for the same reason. Of course, Norman does not believe these things, preferring to think that Tansy's neuroses have taken a rather unusual but not particularly significant direction; this, as well as Tansy's uncertainty about the effectiveness of what she has done, helps a good deal in maintaining the sense of verisimilitude so necessary to this kind of exploration. Thematically, Tansy's motivation in her practice of magic and her suggestion that women constitute a secret society in the practice of magic because they are closer to the basics of life will later be reinforced and expanded in a variety of ways. Also, the distinction between black magic and white magic will also take on greater importance as the novel progresses. Thus the three wives constitute the force against which the Saylors must struggle throughout the book. At this point the action proper is ready to start.

Beginning half-way through Chapter Three and continuing on through Chapter Ten, Norman's rationalistic approach to the question of magic is put to the test through a series of experiences that can be explained in two ways. The first two incidents happen almost within minutes after Norman has found and burned the last of the protective "hands" that Tansy has hidden. First, a student whom he flunked the previous semester calls, accusing Norman of conspiring against him. Then, a girl calls, offering Norman her body and proclaiming her passion for him. Although he is upset, he dismisses both his callers without great concern. However, the way that he interprets these two incidents is symptomatic: first, he considers the possibility that they might be somehow related to the burning of the "hands," but then he dismisses this as sheer coincidence. In nearly every crisis thereafter, Norman tends to dismiss the possible reality of magic and witchcraft; even later when he uses it himself, he rationalizes its use as the only way to fight psychologically unstable women who believe they are witches. This is not to say, however, that the things which happen do not have an effect on Norman, particularly on an emotional level. Most of these problems are not major and do not seem particularly significant when listed; nevertheless, their context in the story, with the reactions of the characters and the descriptions of the situations, does a great deal to move the reader toward accepting the possibility that magic is indeed being worked against Norman. Furthermore, the sheer number of things that go wrong, after it has been established that life has been rather uneventful, adds to the feeling that Norman may finally be right when he wonders if these events might be manifestations of witchcraft; but always he dismisses these thoughts as unscientific and absurd (some of his dismissals, however, are weaker than others). In addition, it becomes apparent, as the unsettling incidents multiply, that Norman is nearly ready to accept the "reality" of magic and witchcraft by the end of Chapter Ten, despite his intellectual inclinations; this, plus the rather lengthy musings he does about magic and about how these events might be interpreted in that pattern, prepares the reader for what is to come. Thus, Leiber spends the first half of the novel very carefully and very gradually creating a sense of verisimilitude for this contemporary tale of witchcraft; the reader, like Norman, is almost ready to accept magic as a valid interpretation of events, no matter what his rational mind says. At the very least, he is willing to read on to see what happens.

Chapter Eleven is something of an interlude, the so-called lull before the storm. Tansy, sensing what has been happening, arranges that she and Norman do some of the things they used to do—drinking and petting. This relaxes Norman sufficiently so that she can work a bit of magic on him: she manages to induce him to repeat the formula which will transfer the hex put on him by Mesdames Sawtelle, Gunnison, and Carr to Tansy herself.

The beginning of the twelfth chapter allows the reader to relax after the emotional peak reached in Chapter Ten; however, by the time we are half-way into the chapter, the buildup toward the novel's climax has begun. Shortly after noon the next day, Norman wakes up feeling much better and very alert. This fact is significant for several reasons. It suggests to us that Tansy has transferred the spell he has been under. Now Norman will be the actor, rather than the acted-upon, through the rest of the book. The transferral also allows the rational, skeptical side of Norman's mind to take over, which is necessary to help the reader accept what follows. Norman soon discovers that Tansy has left home, leaving behind only a fragment of paper, nearly covered with ink stains, giving him the first part of a set of directions for rescuing her and some rather cryptic explanations of what has happened. Twice, in a fairly short time, letters arrive which contain more instructions, but the concluding part of the instructions is still missing. Rationalizing that if he found her insane or hysterical the required materials (dirt, cloth, needle, etc.) might pacify her, he collects, faithfully, what her instructions call for. He traces her, follows her, and finds her, only to have her refuse to recognize him; however, the last part of the instructions flutters from her hand. He also catches a momentary glimpse of something huge and dark behind her. As he scuffles with several men who think he is bothering Tansy, she disappears. His only recourse seems to be to follow the directions she has given him, which he does, even sneaking into the cementary for some dirt from a grave. The description of his step-by-step progress through the spell gives the impression that powerful forces are involved and trying to stop him; this is done quite effectively. He succeeds in finishing the magical spell, but he is, by one minute, too late; Tansy's zombie-like body is returned to him, animated only by the desire to be reunited with its soul. This body is capable of most normal actions, including repetition of information; however, it has no spark of life and cannot be said to think. From this point to the end of the novel, the major actions are confrontations with Evelyn Sawtelle, Hulda Gunnison, and finally Mrs. Carr, with the result that at the end of the novel Tansy's soul and her body are united. There are several interesting things about this last section. First, note the skill with which Leiber keeps his audience from rejecting a rather difficult-to-accept idea; Norman's attitude, the mundane setting, and the early preparation have much to do with that, but people's reactions to Tansy are also very effective. Second, there are the long passages in which Norman brings together the information that he has about magic, constructs a theory which interprets the events which have happened in terms of magic, and makes several tentative predictions on the basis of this theory. This is a pure application of the scientific method, the verification for which comes when he is able to create a formula and a situation which work together to return Tansy's soul to her body. Finally, there is the fact that he and Professor Carr (who only manipulates the symbols without knowing what they refer to) create workable generalized magical formulas through the application of symbolic logic to a variety of specific formulas from various cultures. These last two points are what brings this novel into the realm of science fiction, for while it is certainly true that the laws of magic are not what we normally consider to be the laws of the universe, Norman's activity stresses that these laws are knowable and that they behave in a consistent manner once the necessary information is brought together. All told, *Conjure Wife* is a masterful, convincing study of the possibility that other forces operate in our world that we are not yet ready to accept.

Finally, there are two thematic points that should be mentioned. First of all, it is suggested that a totally rational, analytical, and scientific approach is not absolute and omnipotent. This approach certainly has a place and a function, as demonstrated by Norman's means of solving the problem. However, it can also blind a person to other, perhaps more basic, aspects of life. Thus, while Norman may intellectually scoff at the idea of magic, he is at least very close to accepting it emotionally; had he not been so rigidly convinced that magic was mere superstition—as compared to the "reality" of "science" and had he reacted according to his emotions and feelings, which are also real, much of what happened could have been avoided. Whether or not one accepts the possibility of magic is of no consequence; to a certain degree, the theme of the novel goes beyond that to suggest that no subject of investigation should be summarily dismissed as unscientific and that a completely functional human being must be in touch with both his rational and his emotional aspects. In connection with this, there is the distinction between white magic and black magic, which seems to depend largely on the emotion associated with the practice; that is, white magic is associated with love and protection, while black magic is associated with hate and a desire to dominate.

The second major thematic point is that women are more likely to be witches because they are in closer touch with their emotions, while men are more likely to be scientists because of their rationalistic bent. Given the traditional roles assigned by our society, it is true that women are expected to be more emotional and less rational, while the reverse is true for men. However, psychologists are discovering evidence that these seem to be the two basic approaches to life and that one's orientation to one or the other has much to do with what kind of life one leads. At this point, this idea begins to feed back into the first, for psychologists stress that both aspects are needed, and should be in balance, for a truly functional human being. Thus, in a deeper sense, both these points suggest that this novel is exploring what it is to be truly human and what one's relationship with experience should be. Although *Conjure Wife* may on the surface be only a study of magic, it does, through this medium, have something of significance to say about the human condition, which is all one should ask of a book.

MISSION OF GRAVITY

Hal Clement

1954

Mission of Gravity probably should have won a Hugo; instead, the novel which won the award for that year, *They'd Rather Be Right,* has long been forgotten, remembered primarily in the histories of science fiction and on lists of Hugo winners. *Mission of Gravity*, however, is still with us, though somewhat difficult to obtain, for it is one of the very best examples of extrapolative hard science fiction available. That is, it takes a number of known scientific facts, creates a world from those facts, and uses the events of the story to explore the implications and applications of those facts. By definition, of course, the story requires that the effects of these facts on humans (or human-like beings) be the basis of the action. Clement's creation of interesting characters and an enjoyable story which still manage to do a thorough job of examining the consequences of his facts is unusual in a work of this sort; too often, characters in science fiction are nonentities and the story is often a minimal excuse for stringing lectures together. Here, however, action, character, setting, and idea are thoroughly integrated, all working equally toward a common goal. Thus, *Mission of Gravity* is science fiction of the highest order, and, in addition, it is good, solid fiction by any definition.

The basic situation is unusual but quite simple. Earth scientists have landed a data-gathering rocket at the pole of a high mass, high rotational velocity planet whose gravity is, therefore, very high but variable. Because of some kind of failure in the rocket, probably due to the fact that the gravity at the poles is 700 times Earth's gravity, they are unable to retrieve the rocket. Near the equator, where the gravity is only three times that of Earth and where a human can survive and function with power-assisted equipment, they contact a member of the intelligent race on the planet and arrange to have him help them retrieve at least most of the information from the rocket, since the humans cannot go to the rocket. The novel thus concerns two concurrent matters, the progress of the expedition from the equator to the polar region, and the exploration of the nature and effects of the planet. The first of these provides the story-line, while the second provides most of the thematic materials of the novel.

The underlying story-line is, obviously, a straight journey-adventure and is not particularly important in itself. What is important and amazing about this novel is the fact that nearly everything related about the planet Mesklin and the effects of its characteristics is an extrapolation from current scientific data and theory; basically, it is not imaginary science or speculative science, except for a few minor details. One of the few imaginary science details is Earth's development of a technology which will allow men to explore the reaches of space. Before the exploration of valid scientific data (which is the heart of the novel) can take place, it is necessary for men to get there; thus, the assumption of such technology is necessary as background—where Clement very firmly keeps it.

Another speculative point is the existence of life of any kind on a planet such as this. There is no particular reason why life shouldn't develop in such a place, however, and its existence is very helpful to telling the story and exploring the idea; it is, therefore, a reasonable inclusion in the novel. Possibly belonging in this category also is the wedding of a nitrogen-methane atmosphere to this high-gravity planet. There is no scientific reason why the two should be linked, but neither is there any scientific reason why they can't or shouldn't be. Thus, this point, while scientifically "neutral," can add another dimension of scientific extrapolation. These are the major aspects of the novel which are not strictly extrapolations; note, however, that none of them violate scientific data or scientific theory as we know it now (partly because Clement avoids explaining just what kind of basis is involved in the space technology).

There is no known example of a planet similar to Mesklin; that is, none has been positively identified as having the characteristics which it exhibits. However, there is record of a possible sighting of such a planet, though in only one instance and at sufficient distance to allow little more than speculation about this example. It may well have been word of this sighting which motivated the writing of this novel. It is not this sighting, though, which is the basis of the extrapolation in *Mission of Gravity:* rather, that basis is the body of knowledge which we have concerning rotational velocity, mass, gravity, atmospheric conditions, methane, nitrogen, and so on. Once one postulates a planet with an extremely high rotational velocity (the day-night cycle on Mesklin is 18 minutes, Earth time), there is scientific reason to believe that it will also have a rather high mass. There is also reason to link these with a basically high gravity.

There is also another aspect of Mesklin which follows from this speculation: with high rotational velocity, the mass of the planet will spread, becoming much larger in equatorial diameter than in polar diameter. Even the Earth bulges significantly around the equator, so that the near-discus shape of Mesklin is perfectly logical and reasonable. This distribution of the mass and the high rotational velocity also have other effects: they will produce drastic variations in gravity (Mesklin's variation from 3 Earth gravities at the equator to 700 Earth gravities at the pole is acceptable scientifically) and they will produce the kinds of atmospheric conditions which are found on Mesklin in this novel. In short, to avoid a much longer list, it is safe to say that nearly everything about the planet Mesklin is not only scientifically valid, but also carefully extrapolated from known data and theory. Mesklin was constructed by Clement through a process something like this: If A is postulated, then current scientific knowledge and theory states that B, C, D, and so on either must follow or can logically and validly follow.

The same process seems to have been used in creating the Mesklinites, both physically and psychologically. Given the immense gravity, the long but not too long, low, cylindrical bodies would certainly be logical survival factors. The length (15″) seems determined by two factors: the neural organization necessary for intelligence would seem to indicate some sort of minimum length, while the tremendous gravity would make the shortest length possible an advantage to survival (consider, for example, the problems a dachshund has with its back). In addition, the number of legs a Mesklinite has would logically be needed to support his weight. The cylindrical shape is also an extremely strong one. Even more than this, however, the shape and number of legs suggest a kinship with some forms of Earth's insect life, a kinship which accounts for several other factors about the Mesklinites. The exo-skeleton seems based on this relationship, while also providing rigidity for the cylinder. In addition, the exo-skeleton is one of the factors involved in allowing Mesklinites to survive comfortably in liquid for a considerable time, for it creates a high surface tension which prevents the liquid from entering the breathing apparatus; this is evident in a number of Earth insects, as is the breathing system of these beings. There are no immediate examples of insects able to draw free nitrogen (or oxygen) from liquid, so that a special metabolism would be needed to do so, as the Mesklinites do; nevertheless, such a system would be scientifically reasonable. By and large, then, the physical factors involved in Clement's description of the Mesklinites seem to be as fully extrapolative as his descriptions of the planet.

With one major exception, which does not contradict science particularly and which does add a great deal to the interest of the novel, the psychological factors in the characterization of the Mesklinites are clearly extrapolated reactions to the conditions in which they live, particularly in relation to the force of gravity. Even some of the differences in psychology (and physiology) of the other "tribes" of Mesklinites whom the adventurers encounter are due to the difference in gravity between locations on this world. For example, the group that the novel focuses on, headed by Barlennan, is from the 700 gravities polar areas of the planet, and one idea that continually recurs while they are in the lighter regions is that it will be pleasant to return to a more "normal" weight. Furthermore, when Barlennan is picked up by Charles Lackland (the Earth scientist who is the primary contact between beings) to be put on the tank, he is terrified; he has every right to be, for a six-inch fall in his home latitudes would be fatal. For this reason, too, the Mesklinites normally avoid even rearing up half their length in order to see or to perform tasks; half of fifteen inches is seven and a half inches, a more than fatal height. Because of this, they also have a great fear of being underneath any kind of solid object; the roofs of their houses are pieces of cloth. Even at the equator, the rate at which an object falls toward the ground is three times faster than it is on Earth, while in the polar regions it is much, much greater.

There is little wonder, then, that Barlennan's people have never considered throwing anything, or devising a projectile weapon, or flying. However, other "races" on Mesklin, who live in the lower-gravity regions, have thought of these things and do not have as great a fear of height or of solid objects, since the lighter gravity allows a slower, and consequently a less deadly, fall. All of these factors, as well as a number of others, are definite outgrowths of the conditions of life on Mesklin. The exception to this, or really the bundle of related exceptions, is the "Yankee skipper" character displayed by Barlennan and the rather adventurous nature of his men. Though not particularly tied to conditions on Mesklin, they do have ties with general human nature, which adds interest and gives the reader something reasonably familiar as background while reading the novel. Of course, given the fact that they are roving sea traders (and a great deal of detail about the possibility and methods of this occupation is provided in the novel, all of it logical extrapolation), it is likely that the group which the reader focuses on will be among the most adventuresome "people" on the planet. They will also be among those with a great deal of experience in meeting unusual conditions, so that their adaptability during the course of the adventure is reasonable. As their leader, Barlennan reasonably exhibits these qualities to a higher degree than his followers, both because of natural inclination and because of his awareness that if he does not exhibit these qualities— if he shows unreasonable fear or indecisiveness—he will be deposed. Furthermore, his linguistic ability and his sharpness as a trader and as a bargainer, as well as his guardedness in revealing everything to anyone, are all necessary qualities to his occupation— or would be if he were on Earth. All his characteristics seem related either to the conditions on Mesklin or to his trade; nevertheless, it is somewhat startling to think of a being fifteen inches long with thirty-six legs in the same terms that one would use for a Yankee skipper in the great days of the China trade. However, it does add to the pleasure of watching him in action, which constitutes a large part of the novel.

Most of the thematic interest in *Mission of Gravity* is focused on the adaptation of intelligent life to the conditions of its world and on the ability to change. There is one further theme that is of particular interest, and a brief—and therefore inadequate— statement of it might be: intelligence begets curiosity and a desire for knowledge. It is made clear, for example, that a major motivation for Barlennan's decision to enter into an alliance with the Earthmen is because he wants to gain knowledge. In his meetings with other groups of Mesklinites, he is always ready to trade, but the things which most catch his attention are the things which are unheard of in his home latitudes. In addition, when he does not understand something, he calls upon the Earthmen for help in understanding it. His first mate, Dondragmar, learns English from listening to conversations between Charles Lackland and Barlennan, simply because he is interested. Finally, once Barlennan realizes that the rocket and the data contained in it are too far beyond the stage his culture has reached either to learn from it or sell it, he forces a re-negotiation of his pact with the Earthmen. What he decides upon is education in the basics of science, the things men learned at earlier stages of the development of the sciences. His desire for this is so strong that he would even be willing to stop selling for profit—the primary motivation in his life until this time—in order to learn himself and to help others learn.

Somewhat related to this point is the tendency to underestimate the Mesklinites, particularly concerning intelligence and the desire to learn; the Earthmen tend to think that weather reports and similar things will be sufficient payment for the job the Mesklinites do for them. They assume Barlennan is completely open with them and are ignorant of his great interest in this task, in spite of a number of clues. They frequently put off questions, in effect saying that he doesn't know enough for them to explain it. While this may be true, and Barlennan realizes it, they don't even consider the possibility of explaining on a simpler level. This attitude, conscious or not, is a commentary on the nature of man in his dealings with others unlike himself.

Though it would take a great deal of knowledge about science, it would take no great skill as a writer to do the straight job of extrapolating from known science on Earth to the conditions on Mesklin. To weave the details which have been mentioned here, and many more, into a convincing portrait of another world takes more skill. To weave all these details into an interesting adventure story with memorable characters while at the same time building a convincing world takes further skill. To do all this without resorting to a great number of interpolated lectures takes yet more skill. This last is what Hal Clement achieved in *Mission of Gravity*.

A CANTICLE FOR LEIBOWITZ

Walter M. Miller, Jr.

Hugo Award, 1960

A Canticle for Leibowitz is an unusual book in several ways, all of which contribute to the continuing interest readers have had in it. It is one of a very small number of science fiction novels or stories which have religion as a primary focus. Furthermore, it is one of those books which people who are not science fiction buffs read in large numbers without becoming disturbed by the fact that they are reading science fiction. A genuine sense of humor continues throughout the novel, something which is not particularly widespread in science fiction. And finally, it is one of those novels, which are all too rare, that grows in depth, richness, and interest through repeated readings. It richly deserves the award and the acclaim that have been accorded it.

The novel is divided into three sections: *Fiat Homo* (roughly, let there be man), *Fiat Lux* (let there be light), and *Fiat Voluntas Tua* (let Thy will be done). Each of these sections concentrates on a relatively small portion of human history, but that portion manages to do a great deal to indicate what direction man has come since the previous section and what direction he will take in the years that follow, particularly since there are clear parallels between the history of man to the present and the future history that Miller projects. The first section takes place about six hundred years from now, the second six hundred years beyond the first, and the third yet another six hundred years in the future; including the references to our own time or to our near future, the scope of the novel is 1800 years of projected human history.

The first section begins simply enough: a young novice of a religious order is observing a Lenten fast in the desert. It is not long, however, before we conclude that this is happening not in the past as one might have expected, but in the future; moreover, it is a future following a nuclear war which effectively wiped out a good deal of civilization. This section, then, works on two levels—the material level and the spiritual level. Ostensibly, this section is about the discovery of some relics of Isaac Edward Leibowitz, the founder of the religious order of the novel, the effect of that discovery on the life of the Order, and the process whereby Leibowitz is admitted to sainthood; the human focus for these things is Brother Francis Gerard of Utah, the novice in the desert who found these relics during his vigil. On another level, and in the course of detailing the effects of the discovery, the reader is also given a good deal of information about the war six hundred years earlier and its effects on the 26th Century. Despite the fact that these two levels are easily discernible, in this first section the emphasis is clearly on the spiritual level, the life of the Order and the life of faith. One sidelight, a product of the interplay between these two points of focus, is a theme dealing with the nature of history and of historiography; in various ways this continues throughout the novel, becoming one of the more important themes of the work.

In the late 20th Century, the entire world was caught up in nuclear war, the result of power politics between nations, the pride of the rulers of those nations, and the minimizing of the effects of possible war and the weapons available. In the aftermath, the survivors reacted against anyone who had had a position of authority or who had been involved in any way in creating the weapons; in a very short time, this reaction spread to the intelligentsia, to anyone who was educated at all and, finally, to education itself. During this period, government buildings, libraries, schools, books, artwork, technological devices, anything that had anything, however remote, to do with the holocaust, were destroyed. There were also the visible reminders of what had happened—the mutants, the destroyed land, the slag and rubble of buildings—to reinforce men in their hatred of learning and authority. By the time of this first section, ignorance was almost total, though active hatred and action against it were beginning to abate; the only vestiges of government were tiny, scattered, isolated enclaves where people had gathered around a strong man for protection. At best, the situation was like the period of our history at the beginning of the Middle Ages, though in many ways the people had not even made that much progress in rebuilding civilization.

Throughout this period, however, the Church had persevered, adapting to the times. Though Rome had been totally destroyed, New Rome had been reestablished in the eastern regions of North America. The Church as a whole had turned its energies once again to preserving and fostering learning in any way possible. The Order of Leibowitz had been founded by Isaac Edward Leibowitz, a former physicist who had turned to the Church in the aftermath of the destruction and had become a monk in order that some of the knowledge that man had so painfully and laboriously garnered might be preserved until some future time when it might again be understood and used. The Order, then, became an organization of bookleggers and memorizers, in addition to its religious duties, dedicated to finding, gathering, and keeping safe any fragments of knowledge; the founder himself was martyred when betrayed while taking his turn at booklegging. By the time of this story, the monks of the Order still search for fragments from the past and carefully spend time in copying the original documents in order to preserve the originals and to make sure that at least a copy will be available when the time comes. They do not, however, understand most of what they are copying and preserving. All of this, and much more, is shown through the life of Brother Francis Gerard. During his Lenten fast in the desert, an old pilgrim helps him to find a stone the right shape for the keystone of the shelter he is building against the wolves; when he removes this stone from where it lies, there is a cave-in which opens up the entrance to an old fallout shelter. In his explorations, he discovers a metal box in which there are some papers and a blueprint bearing the name of I. E. Leibowitz. There is excitement about the find throughout the abbey, and Francis himself succumbs somewhat to the fanciful interpretations of his experience (for example, some brothers surmise that the old pilgrim may be Leibowitz himself). Because the abbot wishes to see Leibowitz sainted, realizes that the fanciful tales and interpretations can only hurt that cause, and knows that Francis will be a key factor in whether or not sainthood comes to pass, he keeps Francis as a novice for seven years, schooling him to restrain his imagination and to keep the facts, as he knows them, straight.

Finally, Francis becomes a member of the Order

and a scribe; since he is allowed some free time for his own project, he works on an illuminated copy of the Leibowitz blueprint, which takes him fifteen years to complete. In the meantime, an advocate for Leibowitz' sainthood visits to hear his story and to explore the ruins, as does a member of the opposition. Finally, Francis is invited to New Rome for the announcement that Leibowitz has been elevated; on his way home, he is killed by mutants for his value as food. He is buried by the old pilgrim who had found him the keystone that started it all. The story is simple, and it doesn't advance very quickly; it does, however, serve admirably to show the condition of the world six centuries after nuclear war and to show in detail the life of faith which has kept some semblance of learning alive during those centuries of resolute ignorance.

By the time of the third section of the novel, the secular world is very much the dominating force in society, with the Church and the Order of Leibowitz struggling to be heard, to influence men's hearts and thoughts—and not very successful. Society and civilization have reached very much the same point that was reached eighteen centuries earlier; it is strongly implied that the only real difference may be that they have held off using nuclear weapons for a slightly longer time, heeding the lesson of the past to some extent. As in the other two sections of the novel, the focus is again on the Order of Leibowitz, specifically on its abbot: The story is even simpler here. Discovering that the radiation count has been rising, and given the fact that governments have been denying any nuclear testing or even the possession of nuclear devices while, at the same time, making threats to each other, the abbot must prepare a

r of Leibowitz has been to do nothing with
vledge that they have; this seems equally
le as a reasonable alternative to pushing
indly with discovery for its own sake. What-
rnatives there might be, this meeting be-
vo opposed approaches to knowledge is the
he novel; the first section provided the back-
or it, while the third section shows the results
eeting. Even while reading this second sec-
ore having read the third, it is possible to
vhat the results will be.

itically, then, one of the major points that the
dealing with is the question of knowledge,
y scientific knowledge, and how to use it;
bly interwoven into this is, of course, the
approach to life and knowledge. The novel,
provides no answer to the questions it raises,
iowing both sides and acknowledging that
e strengths and weaknesses in this area. The
is not to give us answers, but to focus our
on the questions, to urge us to give these
s some thought, for once one is aware of the
, the process of modification has already be-
, incidentally, the presence of these questions
ways in which they are handled in the novel
of great importance in considering this
be science fiction. Of course, the fact that it is
ion of the results of trends current at the time
vritten (and still are current, though in a
odified fashion) is also necessary and im-
 this consideration. This projection also adds
ematic complexity, for the fact that it essen-
eats past history suggests a number of things
nature of man—his stubbornness, his pride,
ible drive for power and for knowledge, his

specially chosen contingent of the Order to preserve learning. This time, however, advance preparation has been made, and the Memorabilia and other works have been committed to microfilm. Furthermore, the Order has been recruiting some of its members from among those who have served time in space, for this time the Order, the records, and even the Papacy—if need be—are going to one of the colony worlds to preserve the heritage. He does two other things: he tries to defy the state-sponsored "mercy-killing" center that has been located near the abbey (that he fails to make any kind of impression in this matter is a strong indication of the relationship between church and state in this era); and he shrives Mrs. Grayles, a two-headed mutant. He dies when the nuclear fires erupt once again; the ship, however, takes off just in time, carrying the Church and mankind's records with them, ready to endure the long wait until someone is ready to use them, if necessary, but making sure that the records and the Church survive, in the hope that next time the end results of that knowledge might be different.

Thus, the second section of the novel contains the turning point from one vision of life and learning to another vision of life; it contains the direct confrontation between representatives of two entirely different approaches. Two major things have happened in the secular world between the first and second sections: although there are still large areas of land occupied only by roving tribes, governmental units have been organized for some time, with one man finally achieving the vision of a united land under one rule (his, of course). The rise of such relatively stable secular authority has also encouraged the formation of groups of secular scholars interested in studying various things, funded by the growing "states." The religious Order of Saint Leibowitz has also changed somewhat, though not as drastically as the secular world. The monks have continued to study the Memorabilia, and to gain some understanding of some of the things it contains. In general, the Order looks forward to the day when the materials that they have preserved can be put to use or can be studied with understanding, although there are traditionalists who seem to be against any change in the way things are done. Specifically, one of the members of the Order, Brother Kornhoer, has been encouraged in his attempts to build a machine that will produce light, the first of its kind since the disaster twelve centuries earlier. Furthermore, although they are unwilling to allow any of their materials out of the abbey, they do make arrangements for one of the foremost scholars of the time to come and examine the manuscripts and fragments with his party as their guests for as long as he might wish to stay. Thon Taddeo very neatly—almost too neatly, though this clarifies the struggle that is to take place—represents the secular scholar, the man who has broken away from the Church and who will accept nothing on faith. He is cold, he is arrogant, and he is brilliant. This confrontation gets off to a bad start on both sides when Brother Kornhoer surprises Thon Taddeo with generated light for which he has managed the machine; the thon accuses the Order of having hidden something so valuable, which naturally offends Brother Kornhoer. Thon Taddeo does not particularly enjoy discovering someone who is advanced in his particular area of interest, though he is excited by meeting someone who can put a theory into practice. Thon Taddeo is also disagreeably surprised when he finds that even his most highly acclaimed work is

only rediscovery. In spite of t
tween these two factions, hov
respect and mutual excitemen
are promised because of this
moment of confrontation, of cl
Thon Taddeo is to leave. H
leader with plans to bring the
trol, has not only succeeded
larger governmental entities
joined battle against the Chur
that learning should be impar
what other men do with it h
science. If this is not possible,
toward those who support him
of course, would have him co
of what he does, the applicati
discoveries; he would also hav
to avoid such misuse. Thon T
discovery as gain and as adv
insists that there is a cost
counted—both in human and
are, of course, familiar with th
in our own world; there may b
that more and more college
the effects of science on socie
between the sciences and otl
One cannot help but feel aft
the abbot and Thon Taddeo,
are, or have been, wrong in
materials and to learning. We
aware of the need to evaluate
scientific discoveries, and had
admit this (or, in our world,
scientists), many of the misu
been alleviated. On the oth

the Or
the kn
imposs
ahead
ever a
tween
crux of
ground
of the
tion, b
predict
Then
novel i
especia
inextric
religiou
howeve
rather
both ha
purpose
attentio
question
question
gun. It i
and the
that are
novel to
a project
it was
slightly
portant t
to the th
tially re
about th
his insati

inability or his unwillingness to learn from the past and from his mistakes, his desire for observable results, and many more. Even the presence of the old pilgrim, the Wandering Jew, throughout the novel supports this point, for the pilgrim who helps Brother Francis find his keystone and who buries him, Benjamin Eleazar, and the old beggar in the Order's refectory are, it seems, one and the same person. The Wandering Jew was supposed to have refused Christ's invitation and, consequently, condemned to wander the world looking for Him until He came again. His presence in the novel both suggests that none of the answers or approaches offered by either the secular or the religious attitudes are those which will save mankind and that once lost, the opportunity to follow the right path is exceedingly difficult, if not impossible to regain. He is, in short, another facet of the questions about knowledge, learning, and the world that are raised in the novel; he is also a means of tying the three sections together into a whole.

Nearly all of the things which have been mentioned to this point have suggested that the novel is a very pessimistic one, that its view of mankind is essentially negative. However, this is not an accurate assessment of the novel, for there are a number of elements which suggest hope and perseverance. For example, the very fact that the ship carrying the Church and the Memorabilia manages to leave Earth to protect and spread man's heritage suggests the Phoenix arising from his ashes, a new beginning—purified and cleansed of the dross of the old. The legend of the Phoenix also suggests that this process of cleansing must take place periodically, at long intervals; however, the suggestion in the novel is that the interval between the discovery of nuclear weaponry and its use to destroy Earth was longer the second time around than it was the first, which in turn suggests that the dross in human nature may be cleansed and purified eventually through such trials. There are also a number of other points in the book which reinforce this view. The escape of the ship, and its contents, also points to the idea that both the teachings of the Church and the teachings of science (and their related discoveries and their interpretations of man and the world) are both worth preserving. It is their particular applications, in both cases it seems, that need to be modified. Adding to the idea that the Order of Leibowitz, with its dual role, is a source of hope for the future, and to the general aura of hope and faith, is the presence of the old pilgrim; he takes up residence nearby for much of the novel, examining the visitors to see if one of them might be the one he is looking for. Even more than that, however, is the fact that even after more than five thousand years of searching in vain, he still has hope of finding the promise that was held out once. Another symbol of hope in the novel is Mrs. Grayles, the old, two-headed tomato woman of the last section. Although the symbolism here is rather complex, and somewhat at odds with other factors related to hope, the basic promise that she symbolizes is rebirth in innocence. Her second head, Rachel, has simply grown out of her shoulder, smaller than the other and not prone to aging, looking as though it is asleep; there are hints at some sort of virgin birth, for it is reported that the records show no sign of this second head at Mrs. Grayles' birth. When the second war of annihilation approaches, Rachel seems to begin waking up; she comes fully alive after the blast, while the Mrs. Grayles head begins withering. Not only that, but the body, which was showing definite signs of aging when worn by Mrs. Grayles, begins to show signs of regenerating. However, she rejects baptism, withdrawing from it, although she recognizes the abbot's need for Extreme Unction and helps him administer it to himself. Her rejection of baptism, together with her innocence, seems to contradict the imagery of the escaping space ship and its mission, for the solution suggested here is a return to Edenic innocence. However, these two systems of symbols do work together by giving man two directions from which he can work toward his destiny; in either case, he is given another chance, a new beginning.

There is, of course, much more to the book than has been suggested here, for it is very rich and complex. If the novel did nothing else, the descriptions of the characters, of the country around the abbey, and of the monastic life would make the novel interesting; these things are treated perceptively, gently, and with a keen touch of humor. The ways in which the sections are connected are worth noting, and the details behind all that has been mentioned here add interest and depth to the novel.

DUNE

Frank Herbert

1965; Nebula, Hugo Awards

For even a casual reader of science fiction, reading *Dune* can be a vitalizing experience. Although there are many good science fiction novels, none seem to have had the tremendous effect that *Dune* has had, at least on younger readers just becoming acquainted with science fiction. It, probably more than any book written up to its time and more than most since, seemed to show the full promise of science fiction. It is not just that ecological matters are important now, although that helps. It is not just the idea of fighting corrupt politics, although that helps (more in 1973 than in 1965). Nor is it merely the love story or the development of Paul's powers or the Fremen way of life or the various disciplines or the exciting sequences of events or the sense of wonder at things beyond our experience; it is not even all these things lumped together. Rather, it is the fact that Frank Herbert has created a civilization spanning many stars, in which all the factors mentioned are parts, in a consistent and coherent and comprehensive work. Few works of science fiction have ever attempted *both* the breadth and the depth to be found in *Dune*.

In its main outlines, the story-line emphasizes the political struggle and the development of Paul Atreides. It begins in political maneuvering, for the Atreides family has been requested (ordered politely but without honorable alternative) by the Emperor to leave the planet Caladan, their ducal fief for many generations, and to take over the governance of Arrakis from the Harkonnens, (long-time enemies) and supervise the gathering of melange. Both the Harkonnens and the Emperor have reason to want to put Duke Leto Atreides in a more vulnerable position so they can destroy him. The active role in this partnership is taken by Baron Vladimir Harkonnen, who has planted a traitor in the Atreides household and who has followers on Arrakis. Thus, before the Duke and his family can get fully settled in and well-defended, Harkonnen forces, including the Imperial Sardaukar in Harkonnen uniforms, storm the castle. They kill many, Leto dying as he tries to poison Baron Harkonnen, capture others, notably Thufir Hawat, and a few escape, notably Gurney Halleck. Paul and his mother, the Lady Jessica, are temporarily held captive but use their training to escape. Dr. Yueh, the traitor who hates what he does, has provided them with a survival kit and sent them toward protection; he has also sent the Atreides ducal signet so that Paul may have proof of his lineage when the time comes. The Fremen, natives of the planet, under Kynes, the planetary ecologist who has given them a vision of the future, help Paul and his mother escape farther and give them an ornithopter. They escape pursuit in a sandstorm, though the plane eventually fails them. After crossing the desert on foot, they are captured by another group of Fremen; although their leader is ready to accept them tentatively, one of his men would like to kill them immediately, in observance of the traditions of the tribe.

Eventually, Paul is forced to fight with this man, Jamis; he does so and kills him in formal combat. This wins his way into the tribe and earns him the familiar and formal Fremen names of Usul and Muad'Dib. Shortly thereafter, Jessica becomes Reverend Mother to the Fremen. As he lives with the desert people, Paul grows in the Fremen ways, leading up to the test of riding a Maker, one of the giant sandworms of Arrakis. After he has done so, he rapidly acquires a leadership role among the Fremen and leads them on raids against the Harkonnen, who have repossessed the planet. Paul also drinks the Water of Life, a poison used in identifying the Reverend Mothers, who have the ability to transmute it; he survives and it brings his powers into full being.

Finally, the need to combat the Fremen raids, as well as various political motives, bring the Harkonnen and Imperial forces in great strength to Arrakis. With the aid of a storm and the family atomics, and riding the Makers, the Fremen, led by Paul, overcome the numerically superior forces arrayed against them. After formal combat with Feyd-Rautha Harkonnen, whom he kills, Paul deposes the Emperor, taking his daughter as wife, though vowing she will be wife in name only. Thus, Paul's revenge for the death of his father is completed, and the novel ends.

One of the most important thematic elements which is to be found in this novel is the development of Paul Atreides from a rather small fifteen-year-old boy to the ruler of the worlds of the Emperium. He is the son of Duke Leto Atreides and the Lady Jessica, Leto's legal concubine and only mate, who is also a Bene Gesserit. The Bene Gesserit serve a number of functions in this society. One of these is to insure that a mixing of bloodlines does occur throughout the system of human space. For ninety generations, this sect has been matching bloodlines in order to produce a male Bene Gesserit, the Kwisatz Haderach, who will be able to see into areas of the mind not open to women. They have also developed a very rigorous system of developing physical and mental control of themselves; to a large extent, this involves knowledge of musculature, the ability to control it, and the ability to observe it and its effects on such things as the voice, the expressions, and the body language of others. They have developed this to a high art, using one aspect of it, the ability to "sense" when another is telling the truth, to become politically important. In addition, the use of the spice melange allows them some prescient abilities, but perhaps more important, they use an associated poison, which they are able to transmute through their control of the body, to provide a linkage with others who have had the same experience and thus to bring a linkage with the experience of the past, as well as to gain access to some portions of the mind below the threshold of consciousness.

Ordered years ago by the Bene Gesserit to produce a daughter, who was to be bred with Feyd-Rautha Harkonnen to, hopefully, produce the Kwisatz Haderach, Jessica rebelled and produced a son for Leto. This, in itself, was unusual, for she should not have been able to disobey (and she—any Bene Gesserit—had control of the sex of the child). As a child, Paul was trained in several ways not usual even for the son of a Duke. In addition to training in the duties and responsibilities of that position and training in weaponry and tactics, both of which might be expected, Paul was trained by his mother in the Bene Gesserit Way and by Thufir Hawat as a Mentat. (A Mentat is a man highly and especially trained in logic and in correlating all the relevant data toward the probabilities concerning a problem; they are also, apparently, trained to reduce their emotional state to a minimum.) We actually see very little of this actual training, though we are shown enough to get some idea of what it involves. These glimpses, however, also show us some of the results that this training has produced. There is one final aspect of Paul's background and personality that makes him distinctive and which must be integrated with these other aspects in the course of his development: he has prescient dreams, dreams about future happenings, that seem to be accurate. Possibly the most important of these qualities and types of training is the Bene Gesserit training and heritage, for this shapes all else.

The first test he must pass in the course of his development is the gom jabbar of the Reverend Mother Gaius Helen Mohiam of the Bene Gesserit. There are two parts to this—a black box which produces pain through nerve induction and the gom jabbar itself, a small, poison-tipped needle held at the neck; the test is for control over mind and body despite great pain, with failure bringing death from the needle. Not only does Paul pass this test, which the Reverend Mother says separates the humans from the less-than-human, but he withstands more pain than has ever been administered previously. Yet the Reverend Mother does not emphasize this; it is as though she does not want Paul to be the Kwisatz Haderach.

The next nexus of Paul's development comes during the night of his escape with his mother from the Harkonnens; they are in the stilltent and the impetus for the necessary integration of factors comes from within Paul in response to the violent upheaval in his life. Between these two points, of course, Paul continues to learn, both formally and informally. His father, particularly, helps him to gain insight into the political maneuvering behind their move, to learn the ways of ruling, and to discover as much about Arrakis and the ways of life there as possible; during this time, Paul is often with his father, both in and out of council. During this time, Paul also begins to impress the Fremen and Liet-Kynes as a possible fulfillment of the prophecy of the Lisan al-Gáib, while his mother also fits into this prophecy, which had been planted by the Missionaria Protectiva of the Bene Gesserit; this is important both for their survival and for Paul's later rise to power among the Fremen. In that time in the stilltent, Paul's Mentat training is the first to come into focus for him, for he sits there with the pieces of information that he has flowing into his mind and being precisely placed into position in the logical construct he is building in his mind. Yet it is more than that, for he also has at his command the details of observation and the patterns of analysis that come from his Bene Gesserit training. It is significant that at this point he knows he should mourn for his father, but he cannot break the hold of his logical precision of thought. Even his mother senses that Paul has, in a sense, broken through, that he sees and understands more now than she does in some areas. Throughout this time, he relates various ideas, realizing many things he did not, and makes plans for the future. He integrates the prescient awareness that is part of his genetic heritage with his Mentat powers and reaches another level of awareness, seeing the available paths into his future.

The next step Paul must take is to reconcile himself with his Bene Gesserit heritage and training; through his struggle with this, he discovers that he is more than simply the Kwisatz Haderach: he is a seed of something new, and he sees the two main ways the future must go. Then, suddenly, he finds that he can, must, weep for his father; the integration of powers and the realizations that he needs in order to survive for the time have been completed. The leaving of the stilltent the next evening is described in terms of a new birth, but the mother now follows the son. Paul's fight with Jamis marks his next major step in two ways: first, he must put his weapons training to practical use while learning to fight without a shield; second, he kills his first man, confronting death directly. Jessica, however, takes steps to make sure that the joy of killing does not become a part of his character. This also marks Paul's acceptance among the Fremen, and from this point on, he learns the ways of the Fremen—that is, the ways of survival in the desert. As he does so, adding this training to his others, he also gains a leadership position among the Fremen, integrating his father's ducal training.

Paul's learning and integration has two culminating points. The first of these is riding the Maker; passing this test marks initiation into manhood among the Fremen, acceptance into the full rights and responsibilities of adulthood within the group. When Paul passes this test, it leads almost immediately to a crisis, for now he has the right to call Stilgar out to battle for leadership, and many would like him to. To counter this possibility, to assume command without killing Stilgar, who is a most valuable man and a very capable leader, Paul must call upon all his training except that in weapons: he must analyze all situations and reactions carefully; he must control himself and his voice in the Bene Gesserit way, using them to gain a hearing for what he would do; he must use what he was taught about leading men; he must act within the framework of Fremen life while modifying it; and he must come to terms with, and accept, the religious mantle that legend and Fremen belief are pressing upon him. When he succeeds in bringing the tribe to a changing of their ways, also succeeding in integrating nearly all the factors of his heritage, he has almost reached his full maturity.

There remains a final step that Paul must take. He must transmute some of the Water of Life that is used in the ceremony which changes a Bene Gesserit into a Reverend Mother; no male has ever done so, but if he is the Kwisatz Haderach then he must do so to claim his full heritage and powers. He does so, though it is only a drop and though he lies near death for three weeks; this, however, is sufficient. The result is not a further integration of abilities and powers, but rather a raising of them to a higher plane. The succeeding steps of leading the Fremen against the Harkonnen, defeating the Imperial forces, bringing the Space Guild to terms, and deposing the Emperor are merely extensions of these three tests, necessary once Paul has integrated the factors of his personality, accepted the mantle of religious leadership, transformed himself through the Water of Life, and claimed his ducal rights. It might be pointed out that this maturation might have been very different had the Atreides remained on Caladan, for every real advance Paul makes is due to either the death of his father or to the harsh conditions and way of life on Arrakis; the process is not inevitable, but rather the product of meeting a series of progressively more difficult tests.

It may be true that the theme of Paul's development is developed at more length and with more detail than many of the others, but it is by no means the only significant theme in the novel. In addition to providing the motivation for many of the actions in the story, the novel's treatment of political power and political maneuvering is also important thematically. At first glance, it seems that the saying "Power corrupts; absolute power corrupts absolutely" might be an adequate summation of this theme. It becomes quite clear, for example, that the main reason that the Emperor is willing to help the Baron Harkonnen destroy the House of Atreides is that he feels a threat from both of these men. Since Leto is the more capable of the two men, he must be destroyed; as a result, he can use this destruction as a threat against the Baron to hold him in check. In short, the Emperor is using his power to preserve that power and to preserve the flow of money from the spice. In addition to this, when it comes to a show-down on Arrakis, the Emperor is most concerned with the court functions that he will have to miss and with the threat to the flow of spice; he does not really think in terms of human beings at all. It doesn't really bother him that only one of the five troop carriers that he sent to the south returned, but he is bothered by the fact that it was old men, women, and children who inflicted this defeat, for this may mean that his power is more threatened than he thought it to be earlier.

Baron Harkonnen is also corrupt and a user of men for his own ends. In a sense, he is even more dangerous than the Emperor, for while the Emperor has all the power available, the Baron would like more than he has, and he is willing to use any means that he can to attain that power. Furthermore, both of these men are exploiters, concerned with taking as much from Arrakis as they can, as quickly as they can. They have no concern about depleting the planet, and as little concern about the men and equipment who do the actual work of getting the spice. It does seem that these two men, and those surrounding them, do indeed fit that quotation.

Opposed to these two we find two other leaders who do not quite fit into that mold. Duke Leto Atreides, for example, is much more concerned about men than about either machines or the spice if a choice must be made between them; some of his plans for Arrakis include ways of making the spice gathering safer, and he is willing to risk his own life to save the lives of men in a spice factory when they are threatened by a sandworm. He also tries to lead by example rather than by fear, by uniting rather than by polarizing. He is not perfect, of course, but he strives to consider the human element instead of abstract theory. He is well aware of the power that is to be gained by building a fighting force equal to that of the Emperor, but he seems to be more interested in using it to preserve a balance than in gaining power for himself. Perhaps his most serious breach of this ideal is when he tells himself that Kynes will have to learn how to speak properly to him.

Another example of a good leader who is little corrupted by the power that he has is Stilgar, the leader of the Fremen. He impresses Jessica immediately with his knowledge of his men, with his way of trying to turn them aside from actions he does not approve of, with his bowing to the voice of the tribe, and with his understanding of many things, including the necessity of change. Furthermore, in all his actions he keeps the welfare of his tribe the topmost concern; he is even willing to allow himself to be killed if this will help them in the time to come. Though he will fight for his power, it is not for the same reason that the Emperor would fight for his; Stilgar will fight in order to ensure that the challenger is fit to take his place as the leader and protector of his people, not simply to keep the power for himself, as can be seen when the young men of the tribe are calling for Paul as leader. Though both of these men—Leto and Stilgar—may not be perfect leaders, they cannot be said to have been corrupted by their power. The real center of this theme, however, is Paul Muad'Dib, the Atreides Duke and the leader of the Fremen. By the time the novel ends, he has greater power than any man has had before. Yet it is not just that he has power over the Fremen, nor that he takes over the Imperial throne, but rather that, with

133

his awareness of the future and the sense of purpose that has been bred into him, both strengthened by his experiences, he represents a turning point in human history, a point which he must try to manage in the best possible way and with the least possible damage to mankind as a whole. This is a great burden, and the only person who senses Paul's challenging responsibility is Alia. Nevertheless, Paul does seem to manage to resist the corruptions of power quite well: he sorrows when he sees Stilgar become a worshipper, he is willing to make the Emperor as comfortable as possible on the prison planet, he feels great tenderness for Chani, and he still shares the Fremen dream of a green planet: there are many other specific examples. However, he is also a realist, and does those things which must be done directly, regardless of who may be hurt. He has the realization that any choice is not between good and bad alternatives, but rather that making any choice may hurt someone; he has chosen the jihad, with the Fremen running wild over the worlds of the Imperium, for he has seen that the other main direction of the future is even worse, even less desirable. Furthermore, he has seen that he has really never had the choice of preventing either of them; all he can do is try to minimize the unpleasant consequences. The choices facing Paul are very complex, and in judging him, we cannot make simple judgments, but rather must take into consideration the situations and the possibilities facing him. Whatever decision is made, it can be nothing as simple as "Power corrupts; absolute power corrupts absolutely."

Although the ecological theme is not the major or the most directly developed theme in the novel, there is reason to think that it contains the idea which gave impetus to writing this novel. Basically speaking, this theme consists of several elements: the nature and balance of the planet as it is at the time of the story; the ways that people have adapted to these conditions, both those who live with them and those who fight against them; and the vision of a green planet, including the ecologically sound plan for gradually bringing this vision into reality. Each of these elements is complex in itself, and only a few basic points can be touched on here for them. Obviously, the main fact about this planet is that it is almost totally a desert, with only very small polar ice caps. Water is a matter of greatest concern, especially among those who have neither the funds nor the political connections to have water shipped to them from other worlds. It is implied that there is sufficient water on the planet to make a change in these conditions, although finding it in a usable form is something else again. At the very least, extremely careful planning and very sophisticated means of gathering this water are needed if any such effort in that direction is to be successful. And, of course, a great deal of care is needed in order to preserve the life that is already there.

The Fremen were not originally natives of Arrakis, having been brought there as slaves; however, they have adapted themselves and their entire life-styles to the planet because of their desire to survive. It is noteworthy, for example, that they are capable of rather sophisticated technology, but that all their efforts in this direction are concentrated on things related to preserving water. Their burial customs, their treatment of strangers, their mode of travel (both walking and on wormback), their stillsuits: all of these things are directly related to the conditions which they face and to the survival of the tribe. Their vision of the future of the planet seems based on two things: their memory of the world they came from, which they keep alive through ritual, and the word of Kynes about how they can make their world a green one. Patience is a survival trait on this planet, so they are ideally suited to the long period of time that is necessary for this plan to work.

It is Kynes who provides the basic plan, the means of bringing about a change in an ecologically sound manner so that needed forms of life can either adapt to the changing conditions or be replaced by other life forms which can serve a similar function in the changed environment; the Fremen supply the devotion to the cause and the particular application of the plans that will make this dream a reality. Both Kynes and the Fremen, as well as Paul and Jessica, realize, however, that the change cannot be complete, for the thing which makes the planet important is the spice, and water is poison for the sandworms who produce the spice in their earliest (half-plant, half-animal) forms. In addition, Paul values the strength of body and mind that are found among the Fremen, and recognizes that in large measure these are a result of the type of life that they have lived. He would also like to see that there are at least areas on Arrakis where their original way of life can be returned to, no matter what other changes are introduced. It might be noted that everything that is said in this novel about changing the planet is ecologically sound and scientifically feasible; the only questionable area is the source of the water that will be needed to start this cycle in any significant way, but this is something that is not gone into at any length and there are suggestions that the planet does have the sources, so that we can accept this without undue strain to our credibility. In a very basic sense, then, these factors which constitute the ecological theme of the novel are responsible for much that happens in this novel.

In arriving at a core question of *Dune*, about the question or the idea around which most other things in the novel cohere or from which they arise, the best possibility seems to be this: how would you change a desert planet in an ecologically sound manner? From this one would have to know the planet itself, the way of life of the people living there, the reason for which this planet is important, and the plan for changing the present conditions. It would not be difficult to infer from this the idea that this is not the only inhabited planet, which in turn would give rise to some kind of political system, some means of travel between planets, a possible conflict between the natives and those who are after the thing that makes the planet of interest to others. This last point would require that the natives who want to change the planet will need some kind of political power if their vision is to overcome the opposition; in turn this calls for a leader of unusual powers. Since none of these conditions now exist, and do not seem likely to exist for quite some time, it is reasonable to set this in the far future. If this is so, then the particular things which make Paul different from most seem to be rather reasonable, or at least possible. In this manner, nearly all of the details in this novel can be brought into a logical structure of relationships growing out of the basic ecological question. In a larger sense, of course, everything that is involved in any system is a part of its ecology, and this is what we have in *Dune*.

STRANGER IN A STRANGE LAND

Robert A. Heinlein

Hugo Award, 1961

Robert A. Heinlein's *Stranger in a Strange Land* is the first of the very long single-volume science fiction novels, the first in a rather small company that includes Frank Herbert's *Dune*, Piers Anthony's *Macroscope*, Larry Niven's *Ringworld*, and two of Heinlein's own more recent offerings, *I Will Fear No Evil* and *Time Enough for Love*. Since science fiction has traditionally concentrated on the shorter forms of fiction, with the majority of published science fiction still in short story form and with almost all the novels under 300 pages, it is perhaps inevitable that these early attempts at considerably longer works have problems with the form; as the pioneer in this area, *Stranger in a Strange Land* shows some of these problems very clearly. On the other hand, these longer novels also have several advantages over the shorter forms, the main one being that it allows a complex idea to be explored complexly and in detail; once again, *Stranger* provides ample evidence of the advantages of the longer form. Consequently, although it is somewhat flawed, it can nevertheless be said that this novel is a significant landmark in science fiction simply because of its length and because it uses the additional length to good advantage. In addition to this, of course, is its subject matter, which has struck an extremely relevant chord among readers; this has made it the best-selling example of straight science fiction yet written.

The basic story-line of the novel is quite simple. Valentine Michael Smith was born on Mars, the son of members of the first expedition to that planet; since all other members of the crew die, the child was raised by the native Martians. Twenty-five years later, the *Champion* lands on Mars, discovers the sole survivor, and returns to Earth with him. For a time he is kept in a hospital room, partly for medical reasons, but mostly for political reasons; he is "rescued" by Gillian (Jill) Boardman and taken to the home of Jubal Harshaw. He spends quite some time there, time which is spent largely in educating him about the way Earth's society operates. Near the end of his stay, Jubal finds a way to neutralize the interest that the government has in Mike, leaving him free from interference. Shortly after this, Mike and Jill leave Jubal's home and tour the country so that Mike can gain a wider exposure to life on Earth in all its facets. After a time, as a cure to what ails us, he decides to found a "religious movement." The movement grows, gains members and generates enemies. Finally, a mob descends upon the hotel where the inner circle of the movement are staying. Mike goes forth to meet them, knowing that they will kill him. They do.

Clearly, this summary of the underlying story of *Stranger in a Strange Land* does not cover most of the significant elements in the book. It does, however, point toward several of the larger implications— the social satire that forms a large part of the novel and the exploration of religion which takes over as the main focus of interest approximately half-way through the book. These two interests will be discussed in some detail later. A third facet suggested by this outline of events is that this story outline coincides with the basic pattern of heroic romance.

In this pattern, which has been used in a great many literary works throughout history, the first event is normally the mysterious and miraculous arrival of the hero on the scene. Certainly Mike's arrival on Earth fits these criteria. He is, after all, the only survivor of the first expedition to Mars, surviving from birth even though all the adult members of the expedition were dead; that he has been reared by the native Martians only enhances this point. Although we only learn of the training he has received from them later in the novel, this, too, supports this element in the pattern, as well as the view of Mike as a hero in the traditional sense of the word. In addition to the unusual powers gained through his Martian upbringing and such elements as his physical attractiveness, his innocence and basic goodness, his trustworthiness, and his inability to tell a lie, Mike also has other qualities associated with the hero: his parents are members of an elite group, he has been separated from them, he is opposed by various forces, and he must undertake a quest, the purpose of which is to gain knowledge so that he may conquer the forces ranged against him.

Although Mike does indeed undertake a quest, it does not entirely fit the traditional mold of a series of tests that put the hero's life in danger. One of the reasons for this difference is the fact that, in a sense, there are two quests involved, with separate motivating forces, though they coincide in practice. The motivating force behind Mike's first quest is the Martian Old Ones—that is, they made the decision that he would return to Earth, "programming" him to gather as much information about humans and Earth society as possible so that they may *grok* us to the fullness and decide what to do with us. Mike is not aware of this motivation until late in the novel, when the Old Ones take the information from him. However, everything that Mike experiences and learns from the moment he leaves Mars until the knowledge is taken from him contributes to the fulfillment of this quest.

The second quest is more personally motivated—that is, once he has the basic rudiments of Earth's social behavior in hand, he feels a need to broaden his experience and to try to *grok* human behavior more fully. Laughter becomes the clearest indicator of his progress in this quest. The facts that he feels a need to withdraw into himself when he first hears laughter and that he is unable to laugh until three-fourths of the way through the book are indicators of his inability to fully understand human behavior and motivation. When the incident in the zoo finally sets him to laughing, he tells Jill that he now *groks* people fully; thus, his laughter suggests that he has completed his personal quest and is now ready to put his newly gained knowledge to work. The fact that both of these quests are motivated by a desire to learn about the external world, about things that most of us learn unconsciously in the course of growing up, helps to modify the traditional pattern. Another modifying factor lies in the Martian education which Mike received, for it permitted him to be thoroughly in touch with his body, his emotions, and his mind, as well as keeping him fully aware of his capabilities and his limitations. Thus, he already has what the traditional quest is designed to provide for the traditional hero—that is, a knowledge of the inner resources which he can call on in times of stress; however, Mike must learn about the world so that he may fully assume his human estate and so that he may most effectively apply his abilities, knowledge which the traditional hero has before he begins his quest. A final modifying element is the fact that there really are no villains in this novel, due largely to what Mike must learn. However, all this really means is that the things Mike must struggle against are examples of human nature and human stupidity rather than personifications of pure evil. Put another way, if Mike is to fully *grok* what it is to be human, he must learn not only what human strengths and human weaknesses there are but also how these are mixed in people. He must also learn of the effects of institutions on humans; those characters in the book who are most fully committed to established institutions—for example, Digby, Secretary Douglas, Gil Berquist, and the police officers—come closest to being villains in the traditional sense, but they are still human and their motivations are still very human. All of these modifying factors are extremely important in understanding this novel, but the basic pattern underlying them provides a direction and guidance for meaning.

While the main part of *Stranger in a Strange Land* modifies the pattern of the quest quite extensively, the last section of the novel, like its beginning, remains very close to the romance in form and content. Because this is a modern novel rather than a medieval poetic romance, there are, of course, some differences in the details and the emphases, but here the similarities seem more important than the differences. In the traditional version, the hero consolidates his position, practices what he has learned in ruling his people as a benevolent king, and awaits the culminating events of his life. These final events include a descent into the underworld, a confrontation with the powers there, and a return with renewed strength of purpose; even in the traditional romance this descent may be more a symbolic event than an actual one. The last event in the life of a hero is his death as a human, which paves the way for his apotheosis, his assumption into divine status. Mike, of course, does not become a king nor does he rule as one; however, he does assume leadership over an ever-growing group of people, and his purpose for doing so is based on what he has learned during his quest: he wishes to help as many humans as possible reach their full potentials and capabilities. While he is doing this, but especially as the end grows nearer, he seems to be aware that his death is a necessary part of what he wishes to accomplish. Mike does not literally and actually descend into hell; however, he does undergo a period of soul-searching, a time of doubting what he has attempted to do. This is brought on by his knowledge that the Martian Old Ones had "taken" the information about Earth that he had gathered; he is also worried about the rightness of imposing Martian concepts on Earth people and about the time factors involved. With the help of Jubal (who serves as a guide figure throughout the novel), he sorts out the various elements, reexamines them, and *groks* to the fullness; he emerges refreshed and strengthened in purpose and direction. He is now ready for his death, which he knows must come. With his death comes his apotheosis, which also acts to affirm his actions here on Earth; presenting this element in the pattern is, of course, a primary function of the last scene in the book.

Although the social commentary and the "religion" that Mike develops are by far the most commonly talked about elements of the novel, they do rest on this narrative pattern and they are shaped by its elements and demands. Perhaps the most noteworthy way in which the pattern does this is by requiring a basically optimistic view of the situation. The hero of a romance has a power of action that is greater than that of ordinary men—that is, he is capable of overcoming obstacles that most of us could not, and he is capable of perceiving possibilities and of understanding things that are beyond most of us. Because he has these abilities, he can lead us out of the situations that our inabilities and our shortsightedness have led us into. Thus, although the government is seen as corrupt in this novel, we also see that it can be challenged and changed; the situation is hopeful rather than hopeless. Involved here, too, is a positive belief in human potential, if it can be realized. Probably the most definite sign of this belief comes at the end of the book, where it is suggested that by the time the Martians get around to doing something about us, they may not be able to. Thus, in addition to providing a general framework for the novel and a level of thematic interest, the romance narrative pattern also sets the direction, shape and attitude for the particular details that fill it out.

The novel is divided into five sections, each dealing with a particular phase of this pattern. On first reading, however, the novel seems to split into two halves that could almost be made into separate novels. That is, the first two hundred and fifty-eight pages seem mainly social commentary, using the familiar device of the outsider to motivate a closer look at things most of us take for granted and to view them from a different perspective than we normally do; the last one hundred and fifty-five pages seem mainly interested in

144

developing Mike's "religion." Of course, there is enough discussion and portrayal of religion in this first part to provide a tie with the second, just as there is ample social commentary continuing into the second part. Nevertheless, on the first glance, the novel does seem to fall into two parts. This first impression, however, fades somewhat on second reading and almost disappears with a third. One factor is the recognition of the pattern of heroic romance, which provides a framework in which both parts can be seen as elements of the whole. Another factor is that a reader begins to see the small details in the first section which prepare for the action of the last part and the small details in the last one hundred and fifty pages that refer back to the first two hundred and fifty. Because these details are so important to making a whole novel, it is worthwhile to look at each of the five sections of the novel more specifically.

Part One, "His Maculate Origin," begins with a quick sketching of information about the choosing of the first human expedition to Mars and the nature of the radio messages sent back until they ceased. This is followed by an even briefer summary of the space program over the following twenty-five years to the landing of the Federation Ship *Champion,* which found the *Envoy,* discovered that Mars is inhabited, and learned that there was one survivor of the *Envoy.* Even here, elements of social commentary are prominent. For the first expedition, four married couples are thought to be the most stable and most sane crew possible. Consequently, we are given an outline of all the fuss and bother that went into finding four couples with the necessary skills who were also mutually compatible; this even includes an arranged marriage to complete the crew. The first comment involved is that, in spite of the pronouncements of the machines as to the compatibility and suitability of this crew, the expedition fails. The second comes, by contrast, for the crew of the *Champion* is all male, as is the first complement of settlers. Only later do we find that the failure of the *Envoy* was due in large part to the fact that the crew may have been too compatible and too incompatible as well; after delivering his wife of a son by Captain Brant, Dr. Ward Smith kills her, the Captain, and himself. This also lays the basis for the later extensive exploration of the functions of human sexual bipolarity and of the mores governing their expression.

From this point to the end of Part One, and on through a large portion of Part Two, the novel takes on the flavor of the spy thriller, with a show like *Mission: Impossible* perhaps the closest analogy. Thus, Valentine Michael Smith is brought to Earth and put into a hospital under intensive care. There is, of course, good reason for him to be hospitalized until his body can accommodate itself to the differences in gravity and atmosphere. However, there is not a great deal of reason to keep him almost completely isolated and under heavy guard. The first breach of this security arrangement is due to simple curiosity; Gillian (Jill) Boardman, a nurse, is piqued that she is not allowed to even look in on a patient in her wing, so she finds a way. In so doing, she offers Mike a drink of water, thus becoming his first "water brother," other than the Martians and some members of the crew of the *Champion*. Ben Caxton, a newsman and a friend of Jill's, enters the picture shortly after this. He wants Jill to help him meet the Man from Mars or, if she cannot do that, to help him get further information about Mike and his visitors. Although Ben is a fairly well-developed character, especially as science fiction goes, his inclusion in the novel is primarily functional—that is, he serves to explain why the government is so tremendously interested in Mike, he provides a motivating force for the action of Parts One and Two, and he raises questions about a number of things as a surrogate for the reader, who is likely to have similar questions and doubts. The action is quite simple, once the motivating force has appeared in the person of Ben Caxton. Armed with evidence obtained by Jill, Ben uses his column to accuse the government of playing fast and loose with the law in its treatment of Mike. He finally forces his way to seeing the phony Man from Mars that the government has taken to palming off as the real one; just after this he is surreptitiously taken into custody by the secret police. When Ben does not appear or get in touch with her for several days, Jill follows his suggestions; she finds Mike, smuggles him out of the hospital, and takes him to Ben's apartment. They are found by law officers and representatives of the government, but when they become violent, Mike's special talents get rid of them. This section ends with Mike curled in fetal position in a suitcase as Jill lugs him out of the building.

This ending is appropriate for this section of the novel; it deals with both the literal and the figurative birth of the hero, and at the end, after several birth pangs, he is leaving the self-contained environment of the hospital for the greater world outside. As the title of Part One suggests, his origin—his conception and birth, both literal and figurative—is indeed "maculate" (the word means stained and impure). First, he is a bastard, the son of a woman by a man who is not her husband; in addition, his conception and birth lead to murder and suicide. That the laws of Earth make him

147

the legitimate child of three people seems ridiculous on the face of it, but at the same time it seems more sensible and humane than our current laws on the subject. Second, Mike's symbolic conception and birth on Earth is also stained and impure. His seclusion is illegal treatment of any Federation citizen, which Mike is in three ways. Its purposes are to keep him from finding out about his rights and to get him to sign some of them away. The imprisonment of Ben Caxton and the methods used by the men who try to return Mike and Jill to custody also stain his origin.

Nevertheless, this is the birth of the hero, a man with unusual abilities. His withdrawal into a catatonic state at will—which the doctor accepts as normal—and the means by which he disposes of the police agents who would harm himself and Jill serve to give early notice that his abilities are other than strictly human. In addition, his readiness to discorporate—voluntary, willed death—his view of himself and others as food, his seriousness about sharing water, and his problems with concepts of our language also indicate some of the differences of perspective that he brings to the situation, as well as setting up some of the elements that are explored later in the book.

The two factors in our society that come in for the greatest amount of comment are the nature of our laws and the lengths to which the government will go to preserve the power that it has and to gain more. However, since both of these threads are carried through Part Two, and brought to a conclusion there (more or less), they will be discussed when more of the evidence is in.

The title of Part Two, "His Preposterous Heritage," suggests that the commentary on various foibles of human beings and their society will be a major focus

and the inheritance laws which leave Mike with
fortune far greater than he could ever use. In the fi
place, Mike is the legitimate son of three people:
mother, the man to whom his mother was marrie
and the man who sired him. Though this is certain
more humane than our current laws, a point which
very clearly made in the novel, legitimacy and ba
tardy are legal fictions, designed more to smooth o
questions of inheritance than to aid actual human
ings. In a sense, of course, the third person providi
itimacy is superfluous: either the husband is sup
ous because he had nothing to do with concepti
giving birth and thus having no real part in t
ter, or the father is superfluous because his rel
ship with the mother is outside sanctioned boun
because the child will have legally married pa
which thus confers legitimacy. To put it anoth
legitimate is legitimate; multiplying it by a fa
of three is legal overkill. Another example of th
of legal overkill is the "Gentleman Adventure
ment which the eight crew members signe
only means of breaking it are illegal. This co
leaves Mike as the heir of all the eight cre
ers, not just his three legitimate parents; in a
to the large income from the Lyle drive,
ance includes a very large block of stock in t
Lunar Enterprises and other fruits of t
of eight high-powered individuals. As Jubal sa
r strange customs which allow a man to ha
which he has not earned and which create t
al and subtle fiction of ownership in the fi
hat his "property" and "wealth" are far, f
an he could ever use, even with the wilde
wastefulness, simply highlights the foolishne
concepts and intensifies the ridicule. As Jub

of this section of the novel. There are two major vehicles for this commentary, Mike Smith and Jubal
Harshaw. Mike, of course, is an innocent as far as
Earth is concerned and if he is going to be able to
function at all, there is much that he must learn. Jubal
was introduced in Part One by Ben Caxton as a possible source of help; he makes his actual appearance
in Part Two, when Jill turns up on his estate with
Mike. He is cast in the role of the wise old man who
guides the hero through his initial difficulties, and he
has the qualifications to fill this role well. He is a law-
yer, admitted to practice before the High Court; he
is an M.D.; and he has received the D.Sc. However,
for quite some time—well over a score of years—he
has foresworn the practice of these professions, earning enough as a popular writer to enjoy himself
thoroughly while keeping most of mankind at arm's
length or better. He is not a misanthrope, but he is a
pessimist when it comes to most human motivations
and human institutions; he does not, however, merely
react to things and events and ideas, but rather bases
his attitudes on as much information as he can get and
on a careful analysis of the available information. Perhaps an equally good way of summarizing Jubal's
character is to suggest that he is a knowlegeable romantic, a believer that there are great possibilities
open to man but educated to the fact that most people's thought processes and most human institutions
are not geared to accepting, much less doing anything
about, those possibilities. Thus, he combines those
characteristics which allow him to protect Mike,
while at the same time helping him to find out about
human society and to take it with a grain or two of
salt.

There is very little action in this section of the

novel. Yet Part Two is the longest section of the novel, and one of the most important. What these events in this section do is to finish off the spy-thriller plot begun in Part One and to provide a framework for commentary on a great variety of facets of American life, as well as for showing Mike's development.

The two things which received the greatest amount of attention are, once again, the folly which the law is capable of and the potentials for the abuse of governmental powers in pursuit of securing and increasing those powers. Each of these points, of course, is the center of a cluster of related points. Directly involved in the theme of the misuse of power are such elements as Mike's isolation in the hospital; the way in which Gil Berquist and his men find Jill and Mike, burst into Ben's apartment, and manhandle them; the way in which Ben is first given the run-around about seeing the "Man from Mars" and then "hijacked" after he has succeeded; the way in which Captain Heinrich tries to intimidate Jubal both over the phone and after he has landed his heavily armed troops all over Jubal's roses; and the way in which the second wave of troops burst into Jubal's house. The men involved in these actions are arrogant, looking on themselves as perfectly justified in whatever they do and as performing their duties efficiently; they yield to the law only when they are forced to, and they yield only reluctantly and with ill grace. That Heinlein uses the initials S.S. for these special forces and refers to them as a secret police brings to mind Hitler's Storm Troopers and the Russian K.G.B., and emphasizes the danger that he sees in a government increasingly removed from the people. Events that have occurred since 1961, when the book was first published, can only be seen as justifying Heinlein's forecast.

Related to this is the virtual inaccessibility governmental officials—the higher you go, difficult it is to reach them, even on matte portance—and their consequent isolation from the people they govern but also from of their subordinates. This is seen very very didactically in the comments about th system, in the process that Jubal must go fore finally reaching Secretary Gene through the "back door," and in Jubal's to Ben that the Secretary General wo have known *nothing* either about Ben's about the methods used in dealing with related facet is the attempt made by Mike to sign a document giving up Mars under the Larkin Decision and that the settlers on Mars have sign over to the government. A third face much of the government's "public" b private: Douglas, at first, wishes to and Mike aboard his yacht, away ears of any sort; then he wishes away; when he can have neither o a private meeting, to take place meeting; and even Jubal allows th Douglas know ahead of time wha The point is that, if Douglas had beyond a very limited number this agreement. The fast shuff Men from Mars, that is necessit out of the government's attem stitution provide one means of governmental operation.

Two primary devices are lousness that law is capable

points out to Captain van Tromp after the money has been given away, money enough to do the things one wants is one thing, but more than that is a different proposition altogether, because beyond that point man begins to serve the money and the problems induce mistrust and fear.

The Larkin Decision, of course, says that the real owners of a planet are the people who occupy it. Perhaps as a means of preventing war there was some sense to this legal fiction. However, when one person becomes a sovereign nation and the owner of a planet, it becomes merely ridiculous; when that planet has been inhabited far longer than Earth has been by a highly intelligent race, then any question of applying the Larkin Decision approaches stupidity and absurdity. Nevertheless, Douglas, as Secretary General, tries to get Mike to sign away his non-existent rights, just as the first wave of settlers were required to sign theirs' away before they left; a great deal of power is at stake, which those who might have it are reluctant to give up. Heinlein underlines his attitude toward this, and toward such matters as protocol and jockeying for position among governments, with his elaborate facade of Jubal insisting on absolutely equal status for Mike at the "small" meeting with Secretary General Douglas. In loving detail, Heinlein shows Jubal going through the motions that will apparently establish Mike's Larkin rights (insisting on half the space, a flag, and an anthem, arranging Mike's standing and sitting, making the most of Mike's speech, and so on—all to the consternation of the officials who had things so carefully planned their way), only to knock these pretensions down and remove any possibility of applying the Larkin Decision to Mars by very publically proclaiming Mike an ambassador from the Old Ones of Mars.

These are the two main targets of Heinlein's social commentary in the first two sections of the novel. Several other targets are worthy of briefer mention. One of these is the power behind the power behind the power; in other words, the one who apparently controls things probably doesn't. In this case, many of the decisions and actions of the government are traced back to Agnes Douglas; among other things, the various governmental agencies obey her as readily as they obey her husband. However, the chain does not stop there, for she heavily relies on her astrologer, Madame Alexandra Vesant, former carnival huckster in a mentalist act.. This chain which leads to basing government decisions on astrology makes things both more foolish and more human; Heinlein suggests, however, that, while astrology may be hokum, it is as good a way to make decisions as any other the government has available. Another of these targets is our attitude toward cannibalism. While Jubal finds it personally disgusting at this point, he recognizes that it has a widespread existence, both literal and symbolic, on Earth; he suggests that we have too many strange customs and practices to reject someone else's strange customs and to label them savages just because they are different in their beliefs and customs. Finally, religion is viewed skeptically in Part Two; since this is related to matters dealt with in more detail later in the novel, this point will be discussed there.

Part Three, "His Eccentric Education," is much shorter than Part Two, but it contains several significant sequences of action. Before these sequences begin, the problem of what to do with all of Mike's mail is dealt with. This leads into Mike's visit to the

Fosterite Tabernacle. It takes them from their greeting by Senator Boone, who is also a Bishop, who guides them through the tourist area into the service presided over by Archbishop Digby and finally to a meeting between Mike and Digby, from which Jubal and Jill are carefully excluded; a good deal of discussion about what they have seen follows, after which Mike retires to *grok* his experiences. Only later do we find out definitely that Mike caused Digby to disappear during that meeting. The event which marks the transition from this first sequence to the second is Mike's introduction to sex as it is practiced on Earth; his first partner is never named, although it becomes clear that after that first introduction, all of the girls willingly share his bed. The second sequence begins when Mike decides it is time to leave Jubal's home, taking Jill, his first water-brother, with him. The main focuses are on their magic act at the carnival, where they are cashiered because Mike doesn't really understand the psychology of the crowd and where Mike gains his first convert, on their stay in Las Vegas, where Mike further studies humanity in the mass and where Jill comes to a greater understanding of herself, and on their visit to the San Francisco zoo, where Mike first learns to laugh, thus becoming human and understanding humans. Just as Digby's disappearance is the culmination of the first sequence of events, Mike's decision to become ordained culminates the second sequence and this section of the novel.

This sequence of events leads directly into the events of Part Four, "His Scandalous Career," and Part Five, "His Happy Destiny"; these last three sections also contain the same thematic emphases, so they can be examined, by and large, as a unit. The action in Part Four is only indirectly an action, for this section presents a conversation between Ben Caxton and Jubal, in which Ben recounts his visit to Mike's nest; Mike is involved only by report. During this visit, Ben observes a number of things that go against what he thinks he believes. In terms of the action itself, the function of this section is to provide Ben with a means of sorting out his feelings and to come to terms with Mike, Jill, and the nest; in terms of the novel as a literary work, this section functions to help the reader understand, and become attuned to, what Mike is attempting, moving the reader from current points of view to more enlightened views in easy steps. Part Five is the culmination of the novel, bringing the sequence of events to an end, though leaving a promise for the future open. The sequence of events begins with Jubal learning, over the news, that Mike's temple has been destroyed and that Mike has been arrested; Jubal immediately decides to go to the scene to offer any aid he can. Though everyone is busy, mostly working on the Martian dictionary, all are serene. Aside from a good deal of talk, the first event of any importance after Jubal arrives is his full initiation into the nest. The second important scene is Mike's confession to Jubal, through which "waiting is filled" for him and he is able to move confidently toward the inevitable end; this confession and the doubts it reveals are reaches into the depths of Mike's soul, the symbolic equivalent of a descent into hell in earlier romances and epics. The third, and final, major event is, of course, Mike's death at the hands of the mob, which also includes Jubal's attempted suicide, the revival of his will to live and continue Mike's work, and Mike's translation into heaven; these last two elements are primary in providing hope for the future, a sense of an on-going process.

The topic which everyone seems to talk about with this book, religion, receives its most complete examination and discussion in the last three sections of the novel. As Heinlein treats it, the entire question of religion becomes a rather complex one, if for no other reason than that he seems to change his mind about the subject somewhere in Part Three. Aside from several brief references, the first view of religion comes when Mike is listening to a Fosterite service while Jubal is trying to make contact with the government. The language is very folksy, very common, and rather unlike the language usually associated with church services. In addition, there is an emphasis on a party and on commercial exploitation in this scene. The contrast between most readers' expectations about religion and these elements is quite large, with the result that this tends to turn us off, just as Jubal feels he should turn off the set. However, Jubal's reconsideration, that this is something that Mike will have to be able to handle, suggests that he thinks that this is not significantly different in essence from any religious service; because he thinks so, the reader is also led to, at least, consider the idea. This comment on religion is broadened when Mike reveals that he didn't know the service was religious, that he didn't understand anything of all that he had read of religion and didn't really know what religion was, and that there was no term in Martian that came anywhere close to the definitions of religion that Mike has read. Jubal's intellectually honest admission that it is just possible that the Fosterites might have some part of the truth is blunted by his subsequent assertion that even if they do, he still wants no part of them because they don't measure up to his standard of good taste. Furthermore, Mike's concept of religion is extremely simple, uncomplicated, and straightforward; it consists primarily of "In the beginning was the Word" and "Thou art God!" The first of these suggests that Earth religions have some notion of religion as the Martians see it, although they have complicated it greatly, and the second suggests the great differences between Martian and Earth religions.

After this episode, the next hundred pages of the novel are taken up by the political maneuvering to get in touch with the Secretary General, locate Ben Caxton, and turn over the guardianship of Mike's money to Douglas, with only the invitation issued by Senator Boone touching on the question in this span. The visit to the Fosterite Tabernacle, made only when Jubal can no longer stall it off, resumes this thematic thread; initially it is in the same vein as the earlier view of religion, but this shifts toward greater acceptance, even though our view of it is never totally favorable. The notion of one "right" religious group, with all the others totally damned, is the first target; it is also frequently mentioned in connection with Dr. Mahoud. At the Tabernacle, the show business touches, such as the angel-messengers flying about with jump-harnesses, the hard sell commercialism, and the gambling in many varieties seem to confirm the earlier view that Heinlein is treating religion satirically, at least as a human institution. The plush seats, the idea of sitting in church to watch football, and the snake dance led by a stripper continue this trend. The first break comes when Jill admits that, even though she is rather repulsed by what she has seen so far, she would like to join in. The real shift, however, comes when we are shifted to Mike's point of view. Though some aspects of the situation disturb him—what he took as an Old One being only

spoiled food—and though the details are totally for-
eign to him, he feels the ceremony as a growing closer
of great intensity, much like he experienced in his own
nest on Mars. Since it has been established that Mike
is able to feel the goodness or badness of something,
this carries a great deal of weight. His view of this
service forces us to look beyond the trappings and to
recognize that they are unimportant or that they are
important only as far as they help the worshippers
grow closer, become parts of a larger whole. Once
this shift of direction has been made, Jubal defends
even the details of the service to Jill, not so much by
saying that the things they saw were good in themselves but by suggesting that they are no stranger
than other accepted aspects of other religious
groups; once again, the point is made that different
is not necessarily bad. (Remember, Jubal is intellectually honest: he may not agree at all with what
they do, but within the limits of not harming others he
will defend to the death their right to do it.) To be
sure, this defense has a somewhat mixed result, for
simply listing the various practices engaged in by religious groups does not imply wholehearted—or even
half-hearted—acceptance of them as good things for
humans to do; rather, Heinlein is suggesting that not
only should we know what it is that we are rejecting
but also that we should clearly understand why we
are doing so (in a different context, this point is made
even more clearly during Jubal's conversation with
Ben in Part Four).

The tour of the country, during which they try a
variety of jobs which put them in contact with masses
of people, that Mike and Jill take after they leave
Jubal's also has an indirect bearing here. Primarily,
this tour has one purpose: to give Mike an under-

standing of the "marks." (It also serves the function of gaining for Jill a great deal more knowledge of herself and others around her.) That is, Mike can actually do "magic" tricks, but he doesn't know what makes people tick, what turns them on and gets them interested and excited and involved. The people in the carnival have a feeling for this sort of thing, and so do the Fosterites; it is a necessary part of what they are trying to do, and it is something that Mike must learn before he can develop his religion. His experiences with the carnival and in Las Vegas, as well as those in the other places that are barely mentioned, provide him with bits and pieces of the knowledge he needs, but it is the experience in the monkey house that gives him that final piece which makes everything come together into a clear, total picture; in understanding the roots of human laughter, he understands the basics of human motivation. This allows him to determine how he would like to help the Earthlings and how he can best accomplish this. It might be noted that the resulting view of humankind is not particularly flattering, but it just might be accurate.

It is pointed out repeatedly that the organization that Mike builds in this novel is not a religion in any essential sense, although the trappings of religion are used in connection with it. In terms of its aims, it would be more appropriate to call it a school of language, for Mike and the other members of the nest seem to use every opportunity to screen the people who come into the temple for those who can learn the language and for the rate of progress of those who are learning it; the primary distinction between the levels within this "religion" is the level at which the individual can, or is willing to, handle the Martian language. It is an accepted linguistic theory, based on the comparative analysis of many languages, that different languages provide different ways of looking at the world which in turn produce different ways of acting on the world; the more closely related any two languages are, the smaller these differences will be, but the less closely related, the greater they will be. One example of this would be the fact that, although the Chinese had gunpowder long before Europe did, the use of gunpowder as a weapon is a European invention; on the other hand, the Chinese developed other concepts which the Western world is only beginning to understand, and then only because we have come in contact with the East. There are many other examples, but it seems to be reasonably well established that a person's culture and language—and these two are inseparable, each conditioning the other —determine his relationship to the world around him, including his actions, perceptions, and attitudes. Thus, Heinlein has taken a currently accepted and supported linguistic theory, extended it to the point of postulating a language and culture radically different from any on Earth, and suggested that the ways in which speakers of language can act on the world will also be radically different.

The purpose, then, of Mike's temple is to draw the curious and the dissatisfied so that a large number of possible recruits can be screened; the publicity that they get certainly does not hurt this purpose at all. The first circle is mainly for the curious and for those who lack the interest or the ability to move beyond their present beliefs and attitudes; however, it is also designed to meet their needs. It is at the second level that the actual teaching of the Martian language begins in a very limited way. However, Mike is not simply running an esoteric language school; although

the methods are never explicitly discussed, this education goes beyond the language to the Martian culture and to a disciplining of the self to responsibly and
skillfully do those things which the language allows,
such as telepathy and telekinesis. Thus, it is both increasing mastery of the language and ability to accept
the discipline which is considered when the members
of the group are advanced from one level to the next;
some are left at each level, having gone as far as they
can go. It should be noted also that, although it was
not part of Mike's original plan, there is some modification of the Martian concepts and even some addi-
tions to them to take into account the unique characteristics of human life; it is his failure to do more of
this that gives Mike his greatest doubts about the
wisdom of what he has been doing. Finally, there is
the symbolism of the services and the elaborate rites
of elevation that are involved in the services of the
temple. Ben implies that they are mere flummery, and
to a certain extent their purpose is to keep the "marks"
interested; however, in a deeper sense, they are necessary to the human spirit, for they clearly, definitely,
and symbolically commemorate a significant change in
the lives of these individuals, as well as moving them
from their old life into a new and different one. The
final step in this process is into the nest, implying
mastery of themselves, of their surroundings, and of
the language; those who have gained the nest are the
ones who will continue Mike's work as it spreads, giving humans the means whereby to protect themselves
against the Martians and to develop a saner and better life for humans here on Earth. Like all religions,
Mike's aims at bringing individuals into unity with a
larger group and at transcending the self; unlike most,

knowledge and a definite model for doing so are provided.

Sex is important as a part of Mike's life and of his nest, but it goes further than that, for Heinlein suggests a number of times that bisexuality is one of the major distinguishing characteristics of human beings and that it is a primary force behind the particular nature of most, if not all, human institutions and activities. Though he thinks it a very important force in human life, this does not mean that he approves of the way that we treat it or of the direction that it has taken in human history. Nearly everyone recognizes the very obvious fact that multiple sexual partners are not at all frowned upon in this novel. However, some of the ramifications of this attitude are sometimes lost. For example, there is no sexual activity other than between those who have shared water, directly or indirectly, that is portrayed or condoned; this "free" sexuality is kept entirely within the nest. Of course, the notion of a group marriage will be repugnant to some, but it must be emphasized that what Heinlein portrays here *is* a marriage, a shared commitment by each of the individuals to all of the others; the degree of this shared commitment is clearly much higher in this unconventional marriage than it is in a majority of our traditional ones. One example of this is Mike's total and complete concentration on the girl he is kissing. Another facet of the sexuality that Heinlein portrays, although not a prerequisite in absolute terms, is a necessary self-knowledge and a realistic acceptance of the nature of human sexuality; though Jill is both relatively accepting and realistic about her sexuality because of her training as a nurse, she learns that there is a great deal more to it than she had thought during her travels with Mike, while Ben, like most people,

163

must discover that he has really not examined his motivations and attitudes at all before he can enter the nest. Finally, this revolution in sexuality is kept discrete—that is, the reader, of course, knows all about it and has it explained thoroughly to him, but only as they qualify by learning the language is this aspect of the "religion" made known to the society shown in the novel: a great deal of care is taken to respect the mores of the society and its individuals until they are capable of understanding and accepting. Thus, while Heinlein does suggest that our sexual customs are repressive and undesirable, he does not simply call for changes in those customs and actions, for he also insists that any such changes be accompanied by changes in attitude and motivation; of these changes, those in motivation and attitude are by far the most important, for they can lead to saner, not just different, sexuality.

Stranger in a Strange Land is a rich, complex novel that covers a wide range of the social ills that beset us; those that have been discussed may be the major focuses of attention in the novel, but there are many others that are simply mentioned in passing, such as our business practices and the idea of having Mrs. Douglas, who has never had or even contemplated having children, speak on Motherhood. However, Heinlein is not just content with social satire and commentary, for he suggests that there is an alternative, that such things can be altered in a more sane direction. Of course, in one sense, this alternative is impossible, for it is not likely that a Man from Mars will suddenly show up to lead us into a saner future. However, this is not the point of the novel, for Jubal has come to many of the conclusions and to many of the alternatives that Mike has, without the benefit of the Martian language and point of view. Rather, through this novel, Heinlein is inviting us to reexamine our society, to try to achieve a different perspective on it, and then to move in the directions this reexamination suggests; the enemy that he proposes is an uncritical acceptance of the way things are and an unwillingness to change. Perhaps even more important than this critical analysis of our society is the very strong injunction to know ourselves, to know not only what we wish to change or not change but also why we wish to do so, what our motivations are; without this knowledge of ourselves and of our motivations, any changes would be likely to be only change for its own sake or to be a disguised form of tyranny, imposing our thinking on other people. Implicit in this should be the fact that it is not necessary to agree with Heinlein as to the direction that sanity lies or in the direction that changes should be made; obviously, he has a vision of what a sane future might be, but uncritical acceptance of his vision would be no better than uncritical acceptance of the world as it is. Because this is so and because he has presented us with a detailed portrait of the world, Heinlein has achieved, with skill and insight, the basic function of science fiction: he has given us an alternative to our present situation which can serve as a model and a basis for our contemplation and analysis of the world in which we live.

THE MOON IS A HARSH MISTRESS

Robert A. Heinlein

Hugo Award, 1966

This novel is an excellent example of both the strengths and the weaknesses consistently shown by Heinlein, though in it the strengths are much more compelling than the weaknesses. The story-line chronicles the Lunar revolution to break the shackles of an oppressive Earth government; this, quite naturally, draws heavily on the American Revolutionary War and is presented in a how-to-do-it form. The plot, the way this story is filled out, on the other hand, is more concerned with examining the way life might be lived on the Moon and with the nature of government, in addition to rather detailed information about planning and carrying out a revolution. It is in his detailing the conditions on the Moon and their consequences for human beings that Heinlein excels; although some of these details may seem dated, particularly because of scientific knowledge gained since the book was published (1966).

What are some of the assumptions and facts that this portrait of Lunar living are built upon? One of the most important assumptions is that any Lunar colony will be underground, in a vast network of man-made caves, rather than above ground in some sort of bubble-city arrangement. Given the costs of sending up exploratory vehicles, and the unlikelihood of immense gains in cutting these costs to an easily-afforded price, this is a most reasonable assumption, for the materials necessary to begin such a colony—digging tools, airlock facilities (only a few), and enough air-support and food-manufacturing equipment to function until a self-sufficient cycle can be maintained—are smaller, less costly, and more easily transported than those required for bubble-cities. This, of course, assumes that no great technological leap will occur; Heinlein's business here is an extrapolation of current knowledge, not a blind prediction of something we have no way of predicting.

A second assumption is that the Moon will be settled by convict labor, with few if any voluntary colonists; furthermore, these convicts will be of mixed nationality, all nations of the world sending their undesirables to this virtually escape-proof prison. This adds credence to the idea that the least possible amount of money will be spent creating and developing the Lunar colony. Both of these related points, of course, have a historical basis, for Australia and America were heavily settled by convicts from British prisons, and both countries have a mixture of national origins. These two points give rise to several subpoints. For example, the ratio of men convicts to women is likely to be very unbalanced; consequently, Heinlein postulates that women will be given greater respect (scarcity increases value) and that a variety of new marriage patterns, as well as a system of mores modified to meet the conditions, will emerge. Historically and sociologically, these seem to be sound assumptions, even though they may never happen in practice in exactly the way that Heinlein has projected them. Another aspect of this is that the reduced strain on the body will foster increased longevity. One more aspect is that physical actions involve either caution or practice. A third aspect is that irreversible physiological change begins within a relatively short time on the Moon, so that if one stays on the Moon more than a few weeks, re-adjustment to Earth gravity will be impossible; on this point, Heinlein is probably scientifically inaccurate, but we should understand that he is using this idea to keep the story moving at a good pace. A fourth assumption is that once institutions are set up in particular ways and with particular functions, they tend to resist any threat to their power and to change only when forced to do so; this, and its corollary—that institutions tend to ignore conditions that might cause change naturally—are the elements which make the revolution inevitable. Most certainly this assumption has ample historical verification, and there is no reason to assume that it will change in the future. The final major assumption is that under certain conditions, certain types of computers may become self-aware and, consequently, sentient. This may seem quite fantastic and, of all the elements in the book, it is the least likely on the basis of today's scientific knowledge. Nevertheless, Heinlein does provide some data and some arguments which have the effect, in context, of allowing suspension of disbelief. There is also the fact that this assumption facilitates, not causes or allows, the action of the story; that is, without the sentient computer, everything in the story could have taken place with some modification, but it would have made the story longer and filled with details that are now rendered unnecessary. Too, the novel would have lost its most interesting character had Mike (a Holmes Four computer) been left out.

On these assumptions Heinlein has envisioned what life in a Lunar colony might be like, what factors might cause a revolution, and how a revolution might progress. Of these elements, the "sociological" portrait of life in the Lunar colony occupies the greatest amount of plot space, although the other elements form the background situation. This is accomplished by having Manuel O'Kelly Davis as the central, viewpoint character. Mannie (or Man) was born in the Lunar colony and thus knows it thoroughly. He is a husband in a "line-family," which allows the reader to see the life of such a family in its day-to-day workings, as well as in its response to trouble and revolution. He is the only Earth-trained computerman in the colony, having struggled against Earth gravity twice to get the training needed. This gives him access to the central computer, which would be important for revolution. In addition, it is he who discovers Mike's self-awareness, and it is because of Mike's request for information that he attends the meeting which draws him into the revolution. Also, because of his knowledge of Mike, he becomes one of the four leaders of the revolution (Mike, Mannie, Professor Bernardo de la Paz, and Wyoming Knott). With this combination of characteristics, as well as his distinctive attitudes and the way in which he tells the story, Mannie is the perfect choice for the narrator of this novel; he is able to show the reader many of the attitudes that lead toward revolution, and he is in a position to give a first-hand account of the step-by-step planning and execution of the revolution. He is also well-acquainted with life as it is lived on the Moon.

Thematically, *The Moon Is a Harsh Mistress* is rich and quite complex. First, Heinlein takes a look at the nature of government (and the people who run it and create it) from several different angles. Basically, he suggests that the less government there is, the better; that once people begin making laws and restrictions, they become over-zealous; that people in government are most often motivated by unenlightened self-interest; and that political institutions are primarily concerned with preserving their own power. Professor de la Paz, a rational anarchist, seems to represent Heinlein's view; he is the theoretician of the revolution, and he believes that each individual must assume total responsibility for himself, his actions, and those of any "state" which he may create. Mannie, on the other hand, is pragmatic; Wyoming is the idealist of the group.

This question of the nature of government is also examined by looking at the Lunar Authority, its governance on the Moon and its workings as a policy-making body on Earth (which is backed fully by Earth government), and also at its effects on the colonists and their resulting attitudes. And a good deal of attention is paid to the process of setting up an independent government for the Lunar colony. In all of these general situations, as well as in other lesser ones, Heinlein offers us various ideas about government and avoids a single-minded view of the issue.

The theory and practice of revolution is another, closely related, area of thematic interest. It would seem that Heinlein supports the right to revolt, at least in specific cases; in this instance, seven more years of the old government would lead to rioting, to death, and to the depletion of the Moon's readily available resources. However, he insists that if it is to be done, it should be done properly, with those in charge aware of the risks, willing to accept responsibility for their actions, careful in their planning and in minimizing (as far as possible) any risks, ready to take advantage of chance situations, and willing to exploit what advantages they have or gain. These points are part of almost all scenes in which any two of the leaders are planning what they are to do or how their plans are carried out.

A fairly minor thematic element, related to these first two, deals with the use of resources. The mis-use of Lunar resources, due largely to governmental authority removed from the situation and concerned mainly with the end-product, will soon cause an almost total depletion of resources, leaving the colonists the choice of revolution or death. Another aspect of this is the failure of people to diversify their efforts, which would enhance the self-sufficient possibilities of the system and reduce the dependence on the Lunar Authority, minimizing the depletion of resources. Mannie's family has done this, showing how it could be done. Another major area of thematic investigation might be labelled "the nature of change." In this case, there is the suggestion that situations and the conditions that people live in will change, and that humans will adapt to these changes, rapidly and drastically if need be, but basic human nature will remain very much the same and the adaptations will modify rather than discard familiar institutions. For example, given the scarcity of women and the need for fairly large families to insure survival, the institution of marriage is envisioned as having shifted from a monogamous pattern to several other patterns. However, the same relations between people that insure success in our marriages are the same relations necessary in any of these patterns, and the family as an institution is probably healthier in this novel than it is today. Or consider the one-sixth gravity of the Lunar colony; men have adapted their bodies, their thinking and their action-affecting judgments to this fact of life, and thus are able to do the same sorts of things we normally do on Earth with the same automatic reactions. The Loonies are so habituated to this that life on Earth is extremely difficult for them. These examples could continue, for nearly every part of the novel shows the changed situation, the adaptation to it, *and* the kind of human response which we can recognize on Earth today.

These seem to be the major areas of thematic concern in *The Moon Is a Harsh Mistress*. Each reader, of course, will be able to add details, as well as other sub-points, to what has been suggested above. He may be able to add other major areas of theme, or to state some of these points in a different way that is more satisfactory to him. Almost certainly he will be able to point out and examine more minor points (one example: attitudes toward sex) that support major points, making a study of the novel more comprehensive and more complete.

This novel, in many ways, is a very fine example of a science fiction novel. Nearly all of the assumptions which it asks the reader to accept are either firmly based in something most readers know about or are explained in a way that permits suspension of disbelief. The novel also achieves a good (but not perfect) balance between the interest in the differences in situation, the interest in process, and the interest in the human reaction. Probably the major weaknesses in this novel are that the action moves slowly at times and that Heinlein's characters are mouthpieces for various theories, explaining often at great length. However, the things that Heinlein explains are interesting, and it is well worth one's while to overlook these matters in order to consider Heinlein's vision of the future.

RITE OF PASSAGE

Alexei Panshin

Nebula Award, 1968

Rite of Passage is a good novel by any standards;
consequently, it should rank high on any list of science
fiction. One of the reasons that it is as good as it is, is
that it operates on at least three levels of significance
while remaining a unified, coherent novel. On the
most surface level, the novel concerns Mia Havero's
rite of passage, the formal procedure marking her
movement from childhood to adulthood, as well as the
changes leading up to that rite and the changes produced by it. On another level, it is the exploration of
the sociology of a closed society, of the *mores*, methods, and means of living within a gigantic spaceship;
it is this level which is primarily responsible for making this novel science fiction. Finally, on a third level,
underlying both of these, the novel is an examination
of the politics of power, of the relations between advanced and primitive societies. These may seem to be
very different matters, but in this novel they are
brought together smoothly and successfully.

Because the way of life and the nature of the society in which she lives provides the background and
conditions for Mia Havero's rite of passage, they
should be considered first. The novel takes place 164
years after the destruction of Earth. By 2041 there
were eight billion people on Earth, and population
continued rising; housing, food, schools, natural resources were all in short supply, and noise and dis-

turbance laws were strictly enforced. The ultimate result of all this was the war which ended the possibility of living on Earth. However, in 2025 the first of the gigantic spaceships had been finished; by the time of the war, eight such ships were completed (one was destroyed during the war) and 112 colonies in 112 star systems had been planted. By and large, the colonies were settled by manual laborers, people equipped to meet a semi-hostile planet and wrest a living from the land. Partly because of space limitations and partly because of the wear factor, most of their equipment was of the simplest kind, with animals substituted for machines whenever possible. The Ships, on the other hand, are populated primarily by the professional people, especially by scientists and technologists; they view themselves as the means for preserving and advancing the knowledge gained by mankind through the ages.

The Ships in which these people live are quite different from our usual concept of spaceships. These are small asteroids which were opened up, carved out, fitted with the necessary equipment for spaceflight and for largely self-contained living, and then closed again. The Kaufmann-Chambers Discontinuity Equations, which avoid the Einstein barrier, allow the Ships to travel faster than the speed of light; this continuity effect also allows self-contained, invulnerable, easy-to-use space suits. (Wisely, Panshin suggests what happens, but he does not go into great detail, a matter which might be impossible to do convincingly.)

Inside the Ship there are six levels. The uppermost level, the Sixth, is deserted, and its equipment used to make things more comfortable on the other levels after the colonists had been transported. The Fourth and Fifth levels are the residential levels. The third level consists of Earth-like areas: one for growing fodder, food, oxygen and some cattle; one much like a very large park; and another where wild animals roam in rugged wilderness; it is here that the size of the Ship is apparent. This level seems to serve three basic purposes: to preserve something of the memory of Earth, to provide an area where space is not restricted in any way, and to provide a place where training for trial can be conducted. The second level is the Administration level, while First is devoted to Engineering, Drive, Conversion, Salvage, and related activities. Access between levels and between points on each level is provided by Cars, which operate very much like elevators with seating arrangements. The residential levels are divided into Quads, each of which has a large, artificial-grass play area and a central meeting place something like a Student Union. Perhaps one of the more poorly realized aspects in this novel is the sense of what the physical arrangements within the Quads are like or of the living quarters; this is not particularly important, but the lack is felt.

The people living in this Ship are, for the most part, like people anywhere, although the social institutions are adapted to the conditions of the Ship. One of the noticeable things is the institution of marriage. People do still marry and live together. However, because people tend to live much longer (probably due to the sanitary conditions of the Ship, the medical facilities, and possibly heredity), the fact that Miles Havero and his wife have been married for fifty years is unusual; twenty or thirty years is more normal. People still have children, though not many and those normally twenty or more years apart. This is due to an intense concern for population control and the recognition that in a limited environment such as this it could soon become over-populated; these people remember the lessons of Earth almost too well. Also a part of this controlled population is the fact that the Ship's Eugenist decides who shall have how many children; this does not necessarily have anything to do with marriages, but rather with matching genes to produce the best possible children. As far as families go, they may or may not exist, depending on personal choice. There are dormitories for children who don't want to live with their parents or whose parents would rather not rear the children. Some children live with their fathers, some with their mothers, and, apparently, others live with both. Husband and wife may or may not live together; Mia's father and mother did for many years, lived separately for eight years, and seem to be planning to rejoin each other at the end of the book.

Another institution which has changed is education; it seems to be almost completely individualized. This is achieved by two means: sophisticated teaching machines and tutors. In this novel, the stress is on the tutor, with the function of the teaching machine merely suggested. Since everyone—or very nearly so —on the Ship is highly educated, anyone can serve as a tutor; there seems to be some attempt to match tutor and student personalities, although this does not always work. The tutor's main job is to make his charges think and to help them develop a methodology for approaching learning and information. With a system such as this, it is not particularly surprising that two bright children, such as Mia and Jimmy, are doing what seems to be college-level work (for us) at age thirteen. In addition to these facets of the Ship's society, there are two others: the method of government and its policies, and the rites of passage. Since these are related to the other major levels of the novel, they will be discussed in connection with them.

The idea of the rites of passage is, of course, not a new one; baptism, confirmation, the marriage ceremony, and funeral services are the rites of passage that we are most familiar with. In societies which do have the rites of passage initiating one into adulthood, however, the main purpose seems to be to instruct the person formally into the mysteries of the group and to mark the time when one becomes an adult. On the Ship, these purposes, as well as several others, are served by the preparation for Trial and by the Trial itself. One additional purpose is to make sure that no member of this space-bound society is totally unaware of planetary living or totally incapable of survival on a planetary surface. Another purpose, which perhaps receives the most comment in the book, is to provide an added check on the population, since a certain portion fail to return from Trial (12 out of 29 from Mia's group, though this is higher than usual), and to ensure that the population of the Ship is the fittest population possible. Whatever else it is, however, the time of the rite of passage is a time of change, both natural and induced.

Rite of Passage introduces us to Mia Havero at the age of twelve. She is small, dark, and intelligent; she has not yet begun the changes of puberty, and she is occasionally bothered by that, especially when her father teases her or when she notices the changes her friends are undergoing. In familiar scenes, situations, and groups, she is quite adventurous and self-assured; however, she is very much upset by changes and by things that she is not familiar with. She seems quite positive about what she believes, usually consistent with what her father believes. Finally, she has a sharp tongue, which she uses frequently, and she has more feeling for, and understanding of, things rather than people, as she points out several times. The novel, then, traces her physical and psychological development from this point to her initiation into adulthood two years later.

This process begins when her father, who has just become Chairman of the Ship's Council, decides that they will move, not only to a larger place but out of the Quad in which they have been living. After the move, the process continues when Mia and Jimmy Dentremont have the same first- and second-hour rooms in school and, also, the same tutor. Each of these "coincidences" has been arranged by Mia's father, who recognizes her excessive reluctance to face new situations and the fact that she has not been challenged intellectually; it is also suggested that her and Jimmy's gene charts match extremely well.

The next step of Mia's "rite" is developed in four phases. First, her father asks her if she will come accompany him to a planet where he is going on business; she is reluctant, but promises to think about it. Second, Zena Andrus (whom Mia dislikes because she is a whiner) encounters Mia just as she is about to explore the air ducts on this new level; Mia, partly out of spite, invites her to come along. They find a vertical duct, something new in Mia's experience, and decide to climb it. Zena becomes frightened about two-thirds of the way up, but Mia talks and helps her the rest of the way. Third, Mia recognizes the parallel between herself and Zena, and decides that she can face a planet for a short while if Zena could sufficiently overcome her fear and finish the climb. Finally, for the first time she sets foot on a planet and meets some "Mudeaters"; she discovers that they think as poorly of Ship people, and have as many wild stories about them, as Mia has of the colonists. She also survives a swim in the bay. Although this exposure to the colonists does not produce immediate results, it does lay the formulation for both actions and changes of attitudes, and Mia does find, eventually, that she is no longer frightened of them. Shortly after this occurrence, two other things happen: Mia begins her growth spurt, and she and Jimmy begin their pre-Trial training, which will take a year and a half.

This training is very thorough and it is completely optional, although hardly anyone ever chooses to do without it. It includes instruction in riding horses, hand-to-hand combat, use of weapons, dancing and needlepoint (for coordination), meeting difficult situations smoothly and sensibly, building shelters, living off the land, parachuting, and many other things necessary to survival in a strange, perhaps hostile, environment for a month. It also includes three days on a planetary surface where it is necessary to build a log cabin and go on a tiger hunt—to the death—with only knives as weapons. The purpose for all this is to prepare a child for survival on a planet, to give him skills and a method for approaching unusual or difficult situations, to introduce him to as many new things as possible to reduce his fear of the unknown and make sure he encounters as few unknowns as possible, and to build his confidence in himself and his ability to handle difficulties. Thus, although the Trial is, in part, a measure related to population control, every attempt is made to make sure that the young people are as fully equipped as possible to meet it.

During the time Mia is undergoing this survival

179

training, other things also happen to her that mark her development. Shortly after beginning her training, she begins menstruating. She and Jimmy decide to have an adventure, choosing to venture outside of the Ship. She learns a number of things from this escapade, one of the first things being the amount of preparation and the amount of cleaning up afterwards involved in an "adventure." She also realizes that adventures are dangerous. And finally, she learns a little more about human relations. Her first kiss comes on her thirteenth birthday, after Jimmy has taken her to the theater. She also learns a number of things from her tutor. Among other things, both he and Jimmy always demand that she defend her ideas. Probably the major thing at this point, however, is her discovery, on her own, that really she is more inclined to be an ordinologist rather than the synthesist she had planned to be (she also discovers that Jimmy is better qualified to be a synthesist instead of his chosen career in ordinology). Each of these things, of course, marks new steps in her physical, emotional, and mental development toward maturity.

Naturally the culminating point of this level of the novel is the Trial. It is also the most action-packed part of the book. Angry at Jimmy for a remark he made about her father, Mia lands alone, though not far from where Jimmy has landed. She chooses to be a "tiger" and move around (the other Trial strategy is to be a turtle and avoid unnecessary movement). She has an encounter with a number of citizens, loses her pick-up signal in the process, but learns that these people hate Ship people and have already captured one; she is lucky not to be turned in. She is befriended by an old radical, who talks with her a great deal about life on the planet and about why they hate

Ship people, as well as teaches her how to talk and behave as a native would. She also manages to find the captive (Jimmy), help him escape, find his signal, blow up the scout ship these people have captured, and avoid capture until time for their "rescue." And she is initiated sexually, by Jimmy, shortly after blowing up the scout ship. She is, obviously, fit to be thought an adult at this point, having survived the Trial. However, her adulthood shows much more clearly in the change in her attitudes toward the colonists.

In form, the government of the Ship is a two-tiered democracy. That is, most decisions concerning the Ship are decided by an elected council. However, for important decisions, particularly on policy and on the application of policy, the entire adult population of the ship must concur (there are about 27,000). In their orientation toward policy, both the majority of the Council and the majority of the population are distinctly conservative and operate on the basis of a power ethic. Several incidents bring this out quite clearly.

During Mia's first trip to a planet, the pilot tells her a fairy tale about two brothers who are sent on a quest for an ogre's treasure in order to determine who should be king; Ned charms the ogre out of the treasure, but Ned brings the ogre home with him, takes the kingship and marries the princess who had been ready to marry his brother. Although no comment is made, this is an accurate portrait of the pilot's view, as well as that of the Council majority and of the majority of citizens. Its particular application can be observed after Mia returns from her Trial. More of the general "colonial policy" is also seen on this trip. On the return, Miles Havero and his assistant are quietly pleased that they have out-bargained the colonists; they believe in doing as little as possible for the colonists in order to make them self-sufficient in all ways as quickly as possible. They comment that it is not their job to watch the colonists' interests for them in the bargaining process. Both of these attitudes are characteristic of political conservatism. At this point, Mia wholeheartedly agrees with her father.

The second case pertains to the trial of Alicia McReady. None of her first four children have survived Trial. Therefore, she decides to have another child, in spite of the fact that the Ship's Eugenist has denied permission. In effect, the argument of the prosecution is that certain rules have been formulated to insure the society's survival; to do so, the rules must be followed exactly. Alicia McReady has made her choice and must abide by it. For the defense, the plea is for lenience. The prosecution wins the case, with the sentence being expulsion from the Ship on the nearest colony planet. This, of course, shows a rigid belief in adherence to the rules—a matter revealed earlier in a comment of Mr. Havero (concerning Mia's tutor): he didn't believe that there should be exceptions to rules—regarding the expulsion of a man who provided his son with extra weapons for Trial—even though the son failed to return. Alicia's trial emphasizes the conservative climate: one makes his choices and takes the consequences. Once again, Mia agrees wholeheartedly with her father and the prosecution.

Finally, we encounter the case of Tintera. The subject which prompted the commotion on the Ship was twelve out of twenty-nine not returning from Trial on Tintera, most of them apparently killed by the natives. However, the fact that the planet has no birth-control policy, that they might be slavers, and that they had obtained a scout ship, together with the widespread prejudice against the "Mudeaters" on the Ship, led to an assembly to decide what to do about the planet. This leads into a debate on the Ship's policy, for Mia's testimony has made clear that the colonists' hatred of the Ships is a belief that they have been cheated out of their common human heritage. The defense points out that lack of knowledge—knowledge that may have been lost since planting—may be responsible for their free-birth and slavery policies, in which case the Ships may be at fault for not providing such knowledge, especially since they claim to be its preservers. Furthermore, it is argued that the Ships should either do something for the colonists or leave them alone, putting the knowledge preserved on the Ships to a truly constructive purpose in either case.

The argument of the prosecution is for maintenance of the status quo, rigid adherence to the policies that have been formulated for the Ship's survival, and that the people of Tintera have made their choice, which makes them a danger to humanity, and must therefore abide by the consequences of that choice: Tintera should be destroyed. The decision to annihilate Tintera carries by six thousand votes. Mia had, early in the book, mentioned that this had happened at least seven times in the past; however, after the Tintera decision, Mia's tutor, who had been a prime opponent of the current Ship's policy, sees some hope of change in the next generation, suggesting that the vote had been closer than ever before. Mia has finally matured sufficiently so that she can disagree with her father. Her experiences gained through the changes she has undergone; her studies with her tutor, especially of ethics; her close contact with the colonists;

her growing self-examination, especially about her relations with other people—all of these things have enabled her to consider objectively the beliefs she has accepted unquestioningly all her life; she finds them lacking. It is this, more than anything else, which marks her maturity.

Each of the three major levels in *Rite of Passage* has some bearing on our lives today. The most obvious is the analogy between the Ship's government and the government of the United States. However, especially if we accept the novel's definition of maturity, the other levels also have an impact. Because we have been shown that the conditions of a society have an influence on the nature of that society's institutions and ways of life, we should also have a means by which to approach our own society and a method of evaluating it. And although our society has no formal rite of passage into adulthood, most of us undergo similar changes as we mature; we can use Mia's progress to measure our own.

THE LEFT HAND OF DARKNESS

Ursula K. LeGuin

Hugo Award, Nebula Award, 1969

The Left Hand of Darkness is a rare book, one which has won acclaim and honors from both science fiction fans and science fiction writers, one of only three books to be so honored (the other two are *Dune*, by Frank Herbert, and *Ringworld*, by Larry Niven). What is so amazing about this novel is the depth and the detail of its evocation of an alien world. While the book has two major focuses (Genly Ai's mission to Gethen and the adventure leading up to and including the trek across the Gobrin Ice), it builds these focuses upon a wealth of detail about a world of snow and ice that is populated by ambisexual humanoid beings. These details include the structure of government, the modes of travel, religions, outlooks on life and the ways in which the humanoids construct social institutions. By the time that one finishes this book, not only has he seen the first "contact" theme handled differently and well, but he has read an excellent adventure and also knows the world and its people thoroughly. Accomplishing any one of these well would deserve praise; to do three of them well should insure the author a permanent place in the roll call of good science fiction.

The basic story-line holding all the facets of the novel together is an adventure story, one which builds very slowly. At the time the novel opens, Genly Ai, First Mobile from the Ekumen to Gethen, has been in Erhenrang, the capital city of Karhide, which is one of the two nations on that world's Great Continent, for almost a year. His mission is to offer alliance with the Ekumen to any or all of the nations of Gethen who are willing to accept it. In Erhenrang, his task is to meet with the king in order to present his proposal, but he has met with many obstacles, not the least of which is political intrigue. The one person who is most interested in seeing this proposal carried through, Therem Harth rem ir Estraven, the King's Ear or Prime Minister, has tried to maneuver things so that Ai will get a favorable hearing. However, on the morning of Genly Ai's audience with the King, Estraven is declared a traitor and banished, and the King refuses to consider Ai's proposal seriously.

The story-line then divides, one plot following Estraven and the other following Genly Ai. For some time, Ai tries to find out more about the country outside of Erhenrang before moving on to Orgoreyn, the other country on the Great Continent, in order to offer them his proposal of alliance. There he is entertained, then questioned by the Free Trade faction, a group which would like to use him to return to power. However, the opposing faction is stronger and Ai is sent to one of the Voluntary Farms, where the lack of food and proper clothing and the drugs that he is given, more than the work that he is required to do, reduce him to a state near death.

In the meantime, Estraven makes his way out of Karhide toward Orgoreyn. An exiled man has three days in which to get out of his country, with no man able to help him; however, the new prime minister has given orders that he is to be killed rather than allowed to escape, and only the sense of rightness and tradition on the part of port authorities enables him to reach his goal. Once in Orgoreyn, he works as a laborer for a time before a member of the Free Trade faction takes him in. Estraven works with them, and on them, to devise ways for Ai's proposal to be accepted, though he has a much greater sense of the danger of his undertaking than Ai has. When he learns what has happened to Ai, he uses blackmail to find out where he has been sent, sends word back to his king, and follows, with a plan for helping Ai escape from the Voluntary Farm. Thus, the stories merge, Estraven rescuing Ai from his captors. After they have regained their strength—Genly Ai weak from the drugs and lack of food, and Estraven from calling on his reserves of strength—they decide that the best course open to them is crossing the Gobrin Ice, a gigantic glacier some six hundred miles across, separating Orgoreyn and Karhide. They do so, battling wind, snow, slush, volcanic ash, and crevices. They travel eighty-one days before reaching a settlement, three days after their supplies have run out. When they have recovered from their ordeal, they arrange use of a transmitter to bring down Ai's waiting ship. After having done so, however, Estraven is reported and killed. Then, in short order, Genly Ai meets once again with the king, concludes a pact of alliance, brings in his ship, and settles down to the business of setting up an embassy in Erhenrang. His final act is to visit Estraven's ancestral home, to bring them Estraven's journal so that it might be incorporated into the family records.

In summary, this story-line is quite simple, giving little or no clues to the richness of the telling. In that telling, the details that are used to flesh out the bare bones of the story give much interest and depth to the world of the novel and the work itself.

For example, the nature of the planet conditions many of the things which happen. This is a cold planet, the entire surface much like the arctic zones on Earth. The only habitable zones are the Great Continent which contains Karhide and Orgoreyn, some island nations in the Sea Hemisphere, and Perunter, which apparently is very close to one of the poles. There are also several large glaciers on the Great Continent. It is believed that only a mere eight percent less solar radiation would allow these glaciers to move together, eradicating almost all life on Gethen. But the main matter is the cold, the ice, and the snow. Transporting goods from one part of the country to another is possible for only a few months during the summer. Any kind of travel is rather limited and difficult for ten of the fourteen months cycle. The Gethens' inventions are designed to combat the cold, although not so much that artificial aids destroy their physiological defenses against it. Their creation tales, their legends, and their myths are built on and around these factors and those who have fought them. And Genly Ai, a Terran, is perpetually cold. The climatological conditions on Gethen thus underlie many of the ways in which life is met and many of the details of the action of the novel.

The other major conditioning factor of the society and of the action is the ambisexuality of the Gethenians. They have a sexual cycle which roughly coincides with their twenty-six-day month. For about four-fifths of that period, they are sexually dormant (in *somer*); beginning about the twenty-second day, they enter *kemmer*, the period in which sexual activity is possible. During this time the Gethenian is capable of becoming either male or female. To develop into full *kemmer*, however, at least two partners must reach this phase of the cycle at approximately the same time, with one becoming male and the other female. Although drugs have been developed which can determine which sex one will be during *kemmer*, most Gethenians do not use them and consequently do not know which sex they will be; one who was a male one time may be female the next.

The implications of this sexual system are very great, and it affects the entire society. The child takes the name and the heritage of the "parent in the flesh," the one who physically carried him and gave him birth; thus, in most cases, the child has one parent rather than two. When a Gethenian is in *kemmer*, no work is expected of him. Marriage is not one of their customs—partly, one suspects, because of the problems of coming into phase together. However, it is not particularly rare for two Gethenians to vow *kemmer* with one another, which is much respected but has little legal status. There are *kemmering* houses, where people who are comming into *kemmer* can gather, with full social approval. The major effects, however, are psychological, particularly in contrast with a two-sexed society like our own (which the Gethenians consider to be perverted). If there is no sexual distinction between persons and if, furthermore, everyone in the population is likely to bear and rear a child, there is usually much more attention paid to what a person is able to do as an individual. There is a great deal in this novel related to our own so-called Male and Female Principles; that is, the male is supposed to be more rational, more analytical, more aggressive, more active, and so on, while the female is supposed to be more passive, more accepting, more emotional, more drawn to concrete things, etc. Although there are problems with labeling these differing approaches to life according to the sexes, they are two psychologically accurate descriptions of ways in which life can be approached, and, whether this is due to cultural training or not, women more often than not embody the Female Principle and men the Male Principle. In this novel, however, the Gethenians are neither male nor female, but rather are both; it is postulated that psychologically they are closer to a blending of these two principles than any two-sexed race could ever be. Thus, their approach to government, to conflict, to any undertaking is more cautious without being timid. They are also likely to be more subtle than direct, more concerned with concrete objects than with abstractions, less concerned with ideals than with results. As a result, Genly Ai has a great deal of trouble understanding their stan-

189

dards of conduct and their methods of approaching a problem. Of course, the Gethenians also fail to appreciate his standards of conduct and his way of approaching things. It is only after Ai has been exiled that Estraven begins to wonder whether or not Ai has understood what he has been told. In Ai's case, he distrusts Estraven and is duped by the Orgotans, who seem to be more open and direct—but are not. It is only after Estraven and Genly Ai have spent time together on the Gobrin Ice that each man begins to understand the other and to appreciate the approach the other takes, together with the strengths and weaknesses of that approach.

Because Ai does learn much about the Gethenian character, and because he learns to cope with the climatological conditions on Gethen, the trip that he and Estraven take across the Gobrin Ice becomes much more significant than a simple adventure; it is an experience which give Genly Ai the physical and mental equipment, as well as the deeper motivation which he needs to carry out his mission on Gethen. Of the things that he learns in this way, the most important is the way in which the Gethenian ambisexuality, psychology, and approach to life are related. He comes to realize—and as he does so does the reader—that this ambisexuality is a far more important factor in the life on Gethen than even the weather, and that this fact must be taken into account if his mission is to be successful.

Another factor in this novel which has a great deal of importance is the exploration of governments and of the related attitudes toward nations and individuals. There are three types of government presented in this novel, with one of those in a period of change. The Ekumen, which Genly Ai represents, is an association of three thousand nations on eighty-three worlds. Its function is to coordinate and to facilitate the exchange of goods and knowledge. In cases of dispute, it serves as a moderator, but it has no coercive powers. Any decisions made are made through council and the consent of those affected, not by any means of consensus or directives. Genly Ai suggests that the Ekumen is an attempt to reconcile the mystical with the political; true, it is somewhat of a failure, but it is extremely successful at coordinating trade, assisting the spread of knowledge, and moderating disputes, for never in its history has there been a major dispute nor has a dispute been left unresolved. This form of government seems to be the ideal, or as close to it as possible, against which other forms of government are to be judged. When Genly Ai speaks of the Ekumen's attempt to unite the mystical with the political, he is speaking of its embodying an almost visionary view of the community of intelligent beings working together on an ideal plane of relationships. The clearest examples to this that we have are the founding of the United States and the founding of the United Nations. Neither of these have accomplished the visions of their founders, nor have they been completely successful in putting the ideal into practice; however, in the attempt they have advanced mankind's well-being, knowledge, and ability to get along with one another, in spite of whatever failures there may have been. The suggestion in this novel is that this is the direction in which mankind should move—that in working together cooperatively, true humanity can be achieved. The two governments on Gethen, which are compared against this ideal, are the monarchy of Karhide and the Commensals of Orgoreyn; these, in turn, are contrasted with one another.

Perhaps the best example from modern history that will give a sense of the government of Orgoreyn is Russia under Stalin, although it is not as severe and there are modifications. The most important facet of this kind of government, as far as this novel is concerned, is the fact that the people serve the state and do so without question. There are several implications of this: unlike Karhide, Orgoreyn is comparatively heavily industrialized; for the first time in Gethenian history (it is suggested that relatively speaking this form of government has not had a long history), an entire nation can be easily mobilized toward a common goal. Consequently, war is more possible at this time than it has been at any time in the history of Gethen. These things, of course, are tempered by the climate (it is hard to traverse the planet most of the year, whether or not the population can be assembled) and the psychology of the people (they are cautious and relatively unaggressive). Contrasted with this is the monarchy of Karhide; here, the king and his advisors do have some power and some control but the unity of the Domains and the Co-Domains is very tenuous; by and large, the people are free to go their own ways without interference from the government. The major fault is that the king can exercise his power capriciously, striking without warning. With this kind of government, Karhide is obviously more difficult to mobilize and less likely to go to war, not only because of the loose organization of the government but also because this system is more likely to encourage traditionalism (which is also abetted by the weather and the ambisexuality).

These different types of government serve several purposes, besides suggesting advantages and disadvantages of each. One of these purposes is to accentuate differences in the motivations behind the actions of individuals. For example, Genly Ai chose to come to Gethen, and to undergo training by the Ekumen, because he has a vision of a united humanity working together; this vision is fostered by the governmental system which he serves. The Commensals of Orgoreyn (the council of thirteen which runs the country) seem primarily motivated by an idea of progress, of political power for their faction, and of personal gain; at the very least, these motives are not hindered by the kind of government they serve. King Argaven of Karhide is motivated by two things—fear of the unknown and tradition; these can be seen as related to the institution of monarchy as it has developed on Gethen.

At this point, it is interesting to examine the conflict between Tibe and Estraven. Estraven has a vision that includes love of his ancestral home, his country and its people, and his king, but whereas in most cases this would be the limits of vision (as it is for King Argaven), his vision also includes the whole of mankind; in this, he approaches the vision of Genly Ai, although he has only faith to build on. Tibe, on the other hand, would narrow a man's vision, direct it away from devotion of ancestral lands and away from an idea of mankind as a whole, toward total devotion to the state and its dictates. He and the Orgotans, are moving toward abstractions centered in power, whereas his predecessor values concrete objects and entities yet, at the same time, moves toward abstractions centered in an ideal. Tibe's determination to kill Estraven as a threat is symptomatic of his attitude, while Estraven's willingness to allow himself to be killed once he has accomplished his task of delivering Genly Ai back to Karhide suggests his willingness to do whatever he can to further the realization of his vision.

In addition to commenting on human motivations and attitudes and on the uses of political power, this contrast between past and present Prime Ministers also suggests something about the individual's relationship with his government. Probably the most important factor considered is the indication that a devotion to a particular government or governmental unit and devotion to humanity are incompatible in their extreme forms, although there is a meeting point where the furthering of humanity can, even must, be achieved through using governmental forms. The Ekumen have tried to devise a government that can serve this end, and Estraven tried to work within his government toward that end. This aspect of the novel, like all the others, is extremely complex and rich in its implications on several levels; this discussion has simply tried to suggest the basic factors in the equation and some of the thematic implications.

A fourth important element in this novel is a combination of Gethenian religions and their legends. Both of these are used as devices in the telling of the story, to foreshadow later events, and both are used to add depth and understanding to the events which happen and to the Gethenian character. Most specifically, Genly Ai's question to the Handdara Foretellers of the Otherhord Fastness indicates early that his mission to Gethen will be successful, and his welcome by Faxe the Weaver into that community foreshadows his welcome when he returns to Karhide at the end of the novel. The legends are used somewhat more subtly in this way, though not always. For example, the second chapter, entitled "The Place inside the Blizzard," tells the story of a man who crossed the Gobrin Ice, returned to Karhide under a different name, and finally lifted the curse he had laid on those who drove him out. Although some of the details are different, in a brief form this is precisely what happens to Estraven later in the novel and is an explanation for at least a part of what he does. Chapter 4 tells of a Foretelling, suggesting to the reader what may happen in the following chapter, and also showing in dramatic form the Handdara belief that the *form* of a question is important, for an answer to a poorly phrased question is not worth anything.

Chapter 9, "Estraven the Traitor," tells of a feud between two Domains and the way that it is brought to an end. Not only is the "hero" of this legend of the same name and domain as the Estraven we know, but also he works toward ending a feud, gaining opprobrium for his efforts; however, this story also suggests something of what will happen after the end of the novel, for it is the son who accomplishes what his father would have done had he not been killed. In these ways we get some idea of what is to happen in the novel; however, these interpolated legends, myths, and religious stories are probably much more important as indicators of Gethenian character. Thus, as mentioned earlier, Chapter 4 gives a concrete portrait of the results of a Foretelling based on two improperly asked questions, which helps the reader to understand why the Handdara wish to show the folly of such asking and such answers and why they value ignorance (to put it another way, why they believe knowledge of abstractions is worthless, since this may be based on the wrong questions). Both Chapter 2 and Chapter 9 give some indication of the laws of Karhide, especially as they relate to banishment. Both indicate some of the factors involved in the sexual nature of the Gethenians and in their sexual codes. The second chapter, in particular, indicates the attitudes toward suicide and the rules concerning vowing *kemmer* between siblings. All of these things are important in understanding Estraven as an individual and as a man working toward the realization of a vision. These two chapters, together with Chapter 17, show also the ever-present awareness of the cold and the snow; according to the old belief among the Orgota, the first beings were created within the ice, which released them as the sun melted it. This creation myth also embodies a persistent belief of the Yomeshta, one of the major religious cults—that is, the idea of being in the middle of time, between a beginning in ice and sunlight and an end in ice and darkness. This idea is also seen in Chapter 12, where it and its ramifications are expressed by a High Priest of the cult. This seems to have some bearing on the larger subject of the book, for it might be suggested that, for the Gethenians, the coming of Genly Ai and the changes that will inevitably follow will be a so-called center of time.

If a part of the larger subject of this novel is the question of wholeness, then the two major religions, the Handdarata and the Yomeshta, also have some bearing on this, for most of the imagery associated with the Yomeshta is light imagery, while darkness is associated with the Handdarata. It seems significant that each of them emphasizes one aspect of humanity and that they peacefully coexist. While the Handdarata are primarily associated with Karhide and the Yomeshta with Orgoreyn (thus having some reverberations on the political theme), this is not exclusive, and there seem to be suggestions that one can accept both positions without serious problems of belief or action. Finally, neither of these religious positions operates quite as we expect religion to function on Earth; both seem to be disciplines, ways of doing things and seeing them, without the elements of belief and pageantry found in the religions on Earth (the closest examples are the Eastern religions). If there is any serious problem with this novel, it is that a number of factors about the religion of the Gethenians are suggested without being fully developed; however, we are given enough to understand some of the effects of these religions on their followers. While the reader might be interested in learning more about these beliefs and disciplines, the story does not demand more detail in this area, and there is little reason for Genly Ai to make special efforts to research this area nor for a believer simply to decide to tell more.

Although this novel has many more facets to it, these seem to be the ones upon which any further structures are built. Through the story of a young diplomat learning his trade while he learns about the people he is dealing with, Ursula K. LeGuin has provided for us a masterful vision of a future, of government, of a unique world that springs to life, and of humanity coming together in a harmony of intelligent beings of very different kinds. It is not simply the vision, but the depth and complexity of her weaving that vision that makes this novel among the very best science fiction available.

RINGWORLD

Larry Niven

1970; Hugo, Nebula Awards

One of only three novels to win both the honors
for science fiction, *Ringworld* may seem at first glance
not to live up to the standards set by the other novels
to win both awards, *Dune* and *The Left Hand of
Darkness*. This first glance is deceptive, however, for
the story-line seems to attract one's attention away,
somewhat, from the wealth of material and ideas
which surround it. As far as sheer story interest and
quality is concerned, *Ringworld* surpasses the other
two, though not by a great deal. The focus of the
material in *Ringworld* is also different from, though
not inferior to, that of the others; that is, where *The
Left Hand of Darkness* particularly and *Dune* to a
lesser extent have a rather tight focus around a single
basic point, *Ringworld's* focus is diffuse, spreading out
to cover a universe in which many things have already happened and in which a great many other
things can and will happen. Once the adjustment is
made to this difference in focus, however, *Ringworld*
has as much to offer as either of the other two.

The story-line which holds all the rest of this speculation together might be called "The Luck of Teela
Brown." Like many science fiction novels, this one's
story-line is quite simple and built around an adventure sequence; it is, however, somewhat more complicated than many. Some background may be necessary to follow some aspects of the story. The general

time of the story is, apparently, quite far in the future, at least a thousand years or so. Man is no longer alone in the universe, for contact has been made with six other types of intelligent life: the Kzins, the Pierson's Puppeteers, the Outsiders, the Trinocs, the Jinxians, and the kdatlyno. All of these are mentioned in the novel, but only two humans, a puppeteer, and a Kzin are important to the story, while the Outsiders add to one of the thematic points in a minor way. The humans are still very much the same as they are now, although Louis Wu is celebrating his two hundredth birthday at the beginning of the book (they have discovered a "boosterspice" that promotes longevity) and Teela Brown is a product of five generations of Birthright Lottery winners. The Pierson's Puppeteers are a three-legged, two-headed, long-necked, maned, intelligent species whose brain is encased at the base of their necks and roughly between the two front legs; their mouths serve as speech organs and as hands. The puppeteers are, as a race, devout cowards who will do anything to ensure their own safety. Nessus, the puppeteer involved here, is insane; that is, he is not afraid, at least in his manic phase. In fact, some form of insanity is necessary before a puppeteer will have contact with another race. On the other hand, the Kzins are the most ferocious race known, though after a series of defeats in wars with men, which reduced their numbers by seven-eighths, they are considerably more cautious than they were. Physically, they are eight-foot-tall, upright cat-like beings, complete with tails, retractable claws, and the teeth of a hunting carnivore. The particular Kzin in this novel is Speaker-to-Animals, who is apparently something like a translator and who is somewhat more reasonable than other Kzins—which isn't particularly reasonable at all.

Another necessary piece of background is that some two hundred years before this story takes place, the puppeteers had sent a human to the galactic core; when he reported that the suns there had exploded ten thousand years earlier, the entire race, with very few exceptions, had left known space to escape the radiation spreading outward from the core—even though it would not reach known space for twenty thousand years. They are travelling at just under the speed of light (faster travel is possible, but they are just totally unwilling to risk going any faster) in the direction of the Clouds of Magellan. They have found a gigantic artifact which their safety demands be investigated, though their safety also requires someone besides a puppeteer to do it. Nessus, Louis Wu, Teela Brown, and Speaker-to-Animals are the ones chosen to do it, each of them because of particular qualities: Nessus for his insanity, Louis Wu because he has survived an adventurous life for two hundred years, Teela Brown because of her luck, and Speaker-to-Animals because of his combination of strength, ferocity, and relative reasonableness.

The beginning of the story, then, shows Nessus bringing this crew together. He manipulates the transfer booths to bring Louis Wu to him. He actually insults four adult Kzins in the worst way possible—he's in his manic phase—but this brings Speaker-to-Animals to the crew. He meets Teela Brown at Louis Wu's birthday party, but it takes some time before she decides she is going along. The price they are being paid for this expedition is a much-advanced hyperdrive ship which can cover a light year in seventy-five seconds; this appeals to their sense of racial survival rather than to any idea of personal gain, but it is effective for all concerned to know that when the other known races, man and Kzin included, get around to fleeing the core explosion, they will need something that fast to escape it.

The first bit of excitement comes when Speaker-to-Animals attempts to take over the new ship on their arrival; his discovery that Nessus has an excellent means of controlling him should he become too threatening or obnoxious modifies his behavior considerably for much of the time. They catch up with the puppeteer migration quite quickly, discovering that they have moved their five worlds, rather than using spacecraft. After a visit to the main puppeteer planet, where they discover more about their destination and where Nessus wins the right to breed (they have a population problem, too) if the expedition is successful, they head for the artifact, a gigantic band constructed around a sun at sufficient distance so that life can exist on the inner side of the ring; this, then, is the "ringworld" of the title. On strict orders from Nessus, they try a great variety of methods for contacting the inhabitants, and explore as much as they can without appearing over the inner surface, which might seem a hostile act; all attempts at contact fail. However, when they explore the system of shades around the sun which produces night and day on the Ringworld, as well as producing power for it, they trigger automatic defenses against meteorites and so on, which partially disables their ship and forces a crash landing on the ringworld. On their flycycles, which they brought along, they then begin exploring this world, trying to find someone who can help them or some means of helping themselves. Their first sight of the natives, from overhead, surprises them, for the natives seem to be human.

Their next encounter is near a ruined city which was once beautiful, with many of its buildings floating stationary in the air. After being requested to perform a miracle, Louis Wu uses a laser; they react violently against this, for they consider fighting with light a taboo. The expedition members, however, escape without much trouble. Later, as they are cruising along, a chance remark by Nessus causes both Louis Wu and Speaker-to-Animals to arrive at the same conclusion: the puppeteers had rigged the man-Kzin wars to push the Kzins toward breeding a more peaceful race, as well as rigging the Fertility Laws to breed humans for luck. It is not safe for Nessus to rejoin them until near their destination, even with his means of control. They barely escape a huge field of sunflowers of a special type which focus light to kill food and destroy obstacles; Speaker-to-Animals is left furless.

Next they find a ten-story castle which is still floating; from it, they discover a bit more about the founders of this world and how life was lived before disaster overtook them. They also make peaceful contact with a priest; however, as they converse, an automatic mechanism fuses their translators because they are operating on a restricted band. Teela is later nearly sucked through a meteorite hole, but her luck holds and she escapes. Then she disappears from contact, apparently within a large city. As they search for her, Louis and Speaker are caught in a police circuit, with no means of escape until Nessus both can and will do something about it; there is no guarantee of either.

However, he does, using his tasp—an addictive pleasure-producing device—to make contact with a survivor of the ramship Pioneer; from her they learn a bit more about this civilization and its decline. They combine the floating power of the building with the motive power of the flycycles and move back toward their ship, intending to stop at the floating castle to retrieve some wire torn loose from the sun screens (they had earlier snapped it during their exploration, and it had followed them down). In the meantime, Teela Brown rejoins them, with a man. They get some of the wire after a pitched battle in which one of Nessus's heads is chopped off but saved. Slowly Louis Wu, Speaker-to-Animals, the still-living-though-barely Nessus, and Halrloprillalar Hotrufan (Prill) make their way back to the ship, occasionally playing god to replenish supplies; Teela and the Man-Speaker have departed, planning to circle the Ringworld (it is a million miles from edge to edge and many times that around; one of their artificially constructed oceans is large enough to envelop Earth). The book ends as Louis and Speaker are towing their ship up the Fist of God, a mountain punched in the Ringworld floor by some huge space wanderer; from there, the rotational velocity of the world will give them the boost they need to start the still-working ramscoop engines of the ship.

This story is quite extended and reasonably complex; nevertheless, it is simply the framework, the skeleton, which is fleshed out by a great many other things. For example, it was mentioned earlier that this story-line might be called "The Luck of Teela Brown." It is that, for Teela is in the right place at the right time so that she is considered for the trip; she falls in love with Louis Wu so that she will decide to go; the ship is shot down so they will land on the Ringworld; they leave the Fist of God, for she must go elsewhere; they meet a number of adventures so that she can learn caution and concern for others; Louis and Speaker must remain trapped in the police circuit long enough for the man who is her perfect mate to find her before they are released. In one sense, then, this story is about the luck needed for Teela Brown to find her perfect mate. This is in addition to the other ways that her luck is shown. Clearly, this motivates a good many of the actions of the story, but it also ties in with a thematic pattern that might be called "playing god."

In the case of both the humans and the Kzins, the puppeteers have played god by deciding which traits they feel most desirable in each species and have then gone ahead and manipulated conditions so that each race breeds for those traits. There is nothing particularly objectionable about the traits they decided on, but rather the fact that they decided and acted at all. The danger of this is clearly seen here, too, for the luck of Teela Brown is not necessarily the luck of anyone else; Nessus, who was one of those involved in the manipulation of Earth's Fertility Laws, loses one of his heads in order for Teela Brown's luck to continue. He had thought to use her luck for his own benefit, and the benefit of puppeteers, but his plan backfired. There are a number of other instances of this miscalculation, as when Louis Wu breaks a taboo by using a laser so that he might appear god-like to the natives, when his translation device fails; in both cases, disaster nearly results. However, they use the ruse of appearing god-like in order to get food and other supplies; this is quite successful, apparently because they are now aware of the pitfalls involved in using the laser and the need for caution. Finally, there is the recognition that it is sometimes necessary to play god, whether one wants to or not. At the end of the novel, Speaker-to-Animals realizes that this is what he must do; that is, against the Kzinti codes, he must allow humans to take the supership, for if he does not, the Kzins will have an advantage which will wipe out the gains that they have made in peaceful contact with others. Ultimately, this is based on a survival factor: if they continued as they once did, they might very well meet a race with an advantage over them which would annihilate them rather than treat them as reasonably as the humans did. Nevertheless, he is not particularly happy about the necessity of assuming this role and this responsibility. If there is any overall direction that this theme takes, it neither endorses playing god nor discourages it; rather, each case should be considered separately, with as much awareness of the consequences as possible, with recognition of motives, with acceptance of responsibility, and with great humility.

A major means of fleshing out the story in any science fiction novel is the description of the worlds and societies it takes place in; in this case, there are three worlds that the reader is given a glimpse of, with the description of the Ringworld being the most complete and the most interesting. Whereas most of the rest of the science in this novel is purely speculative, trying to guess what kinds of things science might produce in the next thousand years or so, much of the data concerning the Ringworld seems mainly to be an exercise in extrapolation. That is, once you grant the possibility of constructing something like the Ringworld, then nearly everything else follows quite logically from it. It is not the theory behind the Ringworld which is to be questioned, for the theory that is given in the novel seems to be valid in terms of current knowledge; it is the construction job that boggles the mind: it is almost impossible to imagine what it would take to build something with three million times the Earth's surface (with a 90-million-mile radius, a million miles across, 600 million miles around, and 600 trillion square miles of surface area, and thousand-mile-high walls).

Once one gets beyond that and related questions, however, many things about the Ringworld are necessary adjuncts. The thousand-mile-high mountains at the edges are absolutely necessary if this construction is to retain its atmosphere, since it is centrifugal force which holds the atmosphere down, and this would have the tendency to force the atmosphere over the edges were there not some significant barrier. (On spherical worlds, there is not this problem, since centripetal force is involved.) Under such conditions, some means of screening the sun to provide night and day would be necessary, and any artificial means (and no natural means are possible if all faces of a world are toward the sun at all times) will produce the sharp distinction between night and day found on the Ringworld; day would always be high noon, and night would be instantaneously and absolutely dark. The earth covering this world would be comparatively shallow, so that an object as large as their ship would indeed leave a furrow down to the metal if it struck a glancing blow; furthermore, this would also allow bare spots if the planned wind patterns were significantly altered. What is said of the necessary strength of the metal, and of the ordinary stresses on it, is valid, even though we know of no way to create such metal (note too that this metal is new to all the beings in the novel except the natives); it is nevertheless likely that some things, travelling at sufficient velocity, could puncture it. In turn, if anything punctured it, the pattern of air currents would be disturbed by the formation of such things as the Fist of God. Likewise, by drawing air toward the puncture, as the Eye storm does, these changes would force changes in the pattern of life. Thus, there are many aspects of the Ringworld which are logical constructs from current knowledge, once the possibility of the construction job is granted.

Of course, much of the science, and many of the technological results, are purely speculative; however, they are interesting and advance the story quite nicely. It might be noted, too, that many of these gadgets are not original with Niven, though the Ringworld itself does seem to belong to him. The super-hyper-drive ship which is the motivation for at least two of the adventurers taking this ship, as well as the ordinary hyperdrive ships in common use, is clearly beyond, or outside of, current knowledge and theory. The transfer booths on Earth and the transfer discs on the puppeteer world, the flycycles and all their gadgets (translators, sonic folds, food-making machines, reactionless thrust engines, medical equipment, etc.), the moving of entire worlds in a completely regular pattern, the floating buildings, the boosterspice and its equivalent on the ringworld, Nessus's tasps, the *cziltang brone*—these "scientific" devices, and many more, are all based on speculative science that has

207

little or no basis in current science and is sometimes opposed to it. It is interesting to note that at least at one point it is suggested that different beings may have developed theories different from those that are known, with the clear implication that the theoretical base determines what results your science will produce; this seems perfectly true, based on what we now know about languages and about the changes in scientific theories over the years. Furthermore, such speculation about the results of future science is a reasonable activity, even if it cannot be logically deduced from current science, and any such attempt at speculation is probably very conservative if we consider the great number of things we now have that were considered impossible, or implausible, seventy-five or a hundred years ago. Thus, *Ringworld* serves what seems to be a fairly consistent function in science fiction: it seeks to stimulate our imaginations as it suggests possibilities and directions for change.

Another very important aspect of this novel that is developed logically out of the story is the relationship between intelligent beings. This operates on a variety of levels, from the personal to the racial (if that is the proper word for beings who share intelligence but are otherwise extremely different). One of the first things we notice in the novel, though it is rather indirect, is the fact that the Earth is unified. Two factors seem to have influenced this—the invention of the transfer booths and the presence of other intelligent beings in the universe, particularly the Kzins, whose aggressiveness would force cooperation in a struggle against them if this were not already the case. There is also the suggestion that this unity came about naturally, even before contact with the Kzins. On a broader level, there is in this novel an exploration of the possibilities of galactic cooperation, for at the beginning of the novel there are seven known intelligent races in the galaxy, and by its end another has been added. The problems of cooperation on this scale, much less any possibility of complete unity, are much more difficult, although the sentient beings known at the time of this novel are basically cooperating more fully than the current nations on Earth are doing. In the first place, there are problems in communication. Even with the hyperwave radio, it takes time for a message to travel light years. There are also language difficulties; for example, although the Kzins can manage human speech quite well, it is impossible for the human vocal apparatus to shape its way around the "Hero's Tongue" of the Kzin. Consequently, it is impossible for humans to understand fully Kzinti culture. Furthermore, each of these races perceives things quite differently from the others; this is due both to physical differences and cultural differences, while the latter is the only significant cause here on Earth. For example, the kdatlyno see only in the x-ray range; the Kzins are cat-like and their sensory apparatus is similar. Imagine too the difference it would make to be able to see an object from two directions at the same time, as the puppeteers can. Finally, there are the complete differences in motivation. A society of ultracautious vegetarians (the puppeteers) and a society of carnivores who are ready to fight at the drop of a hat, regardless of circumstances (the Kzin) are going to have some difficulties in getting along; the threat posed by the Kzin to their safety led the puppeteers to manipulate the man-Kzin wars, while their belief that an even more lucky humanity would be helpful to them led to their manipulation of the Fertility Laws. It may be true, in fact, that the puppeteers will never be able to make contact with other races except on their own terms; this can be accepted, however, at least partially, because many of their products are far superior to those manufactured by others.

It is between man and Kzin that the greatest strides toward mutual respect and cooperation are made in this novel. At the beginning, Louis Wu and Speaker-to-Animals are both ready to take offense from the other; they also begin by working at cross purposes. Gradually, however, each learns the strengths of the other and each recognizes that these strengths used in tandem can make the expedition safer and more productive, especially if the strengths of one can modify the weaknesses of the other. This culminates in Speaker's recognition and admission that there is much more to be gained by letting men take the lead in the use and development of the super-hyperdrive, and in continuing to allow his race to learn caution and cooperation.

Ringworld is rich and full, with a wealth of ideas and details. There are many details that add to the depth and breadth of the novel; one excellent example is that Prill was, in effect, the ship's whore among her own people, but she is more cultured and has a wider knowledge in many areas than the other characters. Or note the irony in the coupling of her comment that there is much that man doesn't know about sex with Nessus' comment that no other sentient creature copulates as often as man does. This is not particularly important in the sweep of the novel, but it is the sort of thing that adds humor, humanity, and another dimension to the novel. In addition to telling a fine story,

Larry Niven has filled in the details interestingly and in a telling fashion. This novel takes a back seat to only a very few others within the realm of science fiction.

Toward a Definition of Science Fiction

Many people seem to think that science fiction is typified by the covers of some of the old pulp magazines: the Bug-Eyed Monster, embodying every trait and feature that most people find repulsive, is about to grab, and presumably ravish, a sweet, blonde, curvaceous, scantily-clad Earth girl. This is unfortunate because it demeans and degrades a worthwhile and even important literary endeavor. In contrast to this unwarranted stereotype, science fiction rarely emphasizes sex, and when it does, it is more discreet than other contemporary fiction. Instead, the basic interest of science fiction lies in the relation between man and his technology and between man and the universe. Science fiction is a literature of change and a literature of the future, and while it would be foolish to claim that science fiction is a major literary genre at this time, the aspects of human life that it considers make it well worth reading and studying —for no other literary form does quite the same things.

The question is: what is science fiction? And the answer must be, unfortunately, that there have been few attempts to consider this question at any length or with much seriousness; it may well be that science fiction will resist any comprehensive definition of its characteristics. To say this, however, does not mean that there are no ways of defining it nor that various facets of its totality cannot be clarified. To begin, the following definition should be helpful: science fiction is a literary sub-genre which postulates a change (for human beings) from conditions as we know them and follows the implications of these changes to a conclusion. Although this definition will necessarily be modified and expanded, and probably changed, in the course of this exploration, it covers much of the basic groundwork and provides a point of departure.

The first point—that science fiction is a literary sub-genre—is a very important one, but one which is often overlooked or ignored in most discussions of science fiction. Specifically, science fiction is a sub-genre of prose fiction, for nearly every piece of science fiction is either a short story or a novel. There are only a very few dramas which could be called science fiction, with Karel Capek's *RUR* (Rossum's Universal Robots) being the only one that is well known; the body of poetry that might be labeled science fiction is only slightly larger. To say that science fiction is a sub-genre of prose fiction is to say that it has all the basic characteristics and serves the same basic functions in much the same way as prose fiction in general—that is, it shares a great deal with all other novels and short stories.

Everything that can be said about prose fiction, in general, applies to science fiction. Every piece of science fiction, whether short story or novel, must have a narrator, a story, a plot, a setting, characters, language, and theme. And like any prose, the themes of science fiction are concerned with interpreting man's nature and experience in relation to the world around him.

213

Themes in science fiction are constructed and presented in exactly the same ways that themes are dealt with in any other kind of fiction. They are the result of a particular combination of narrator, story, plot, character, setting, and language. In short, the reasons for reading and enjoying science fiction, and the ways of studying and analyzing it, are basically the same as they would be for any other story or novel.

There remains, however, the fact that science fiction is distinguishable from other kinds of fiction. The very title of the genre would suggest that the distinguishing factor is the presence of some kind of science and/or the technology resulting from that science, but it is a particular view or handling of science that is involved in science fiction. For example, in 1925 Sinclair Lewis published *Arrowsmith*, a novel about a scientist who makes a scientific discovery, but *Arrowsmith* is not science fiction. The major reason for this is due to Lewis' concern with *current* science. The story is set in America, in the early 1900s, and the discovery of the cure is thoroughly grounded in the bacteriology and epidemiology of the time. The distinction is this: the science in science fiction is either not current science or it is not applied in a current situation; rather it is extrapolated, carried beyond the current state of the sciences or the current situation, in some way. In *The Andromeda Strain*, for example, the scientific techniques that are used and the scientific knowledge that is involved are essentially current, with very little if any extrapolation; however, the situation in which the science and technology are used, including some aspects of the setting, is a situation which has not yet faced mankind; we have not yet had to deal with a deadly, mutated virus that is brought to Earth by a returning space probe. Consequently, *The Andromeda Strain* is science fiction because of the extrapolation, plus the scientific basis for the action.

Consequently, we can say that the "science" in science fiction is extrapolated science rather than current science; that is, the writer begins from the current state of the sciences and projects what seems to him to be a logical development beyond that current state of knowledge. When most people think of science, they think of biology, chemistry, and physics, together with their sub-branches (zoology, botany, etc.) and their combinations (biochemistry, for example), as well as the attendant technology. It is probably true that a good deal of early science fiction was based on science in this sense, particularly on physics and on technological development. However, over the years, new developments have occurred and new concerns of both writers and readers have surfaced; "science" in science fiction has broadened and changed. Novels and short stories dealing with such things as linguistics, political science, mythology, historiography, religion, sociology, psychology, ecology, and so on have not only been written and accepted, but also have won awards given by science fiction fans and writers. At the very least, this means that the concept of science as it applies to science fiction will have to be revalued and redefined to cover a broader spectrum of ways of knowing about our human nature and environment. However, this step seems a bit drastic, for there seem to be several senses in which the idea of science still applies to most novels and stories that are considered to be science fiction.

Another use of the word "science" (in science fiction) includes what might be called scientific "gadgets." These are devices, large or small, whose development depends on a state of science and technology that is advanced beyond the current state. For example, in *Babel-17* by Samuel R. Delany, the main concern of the book is the examination of the nature, characteristics, and results of an artificially-constructed language; nevertheless, as a matter of course it includes, as part of the background, faster-than-light travel, a technique for reviving certain kinds of suicides, cosmetisurgery, and biological tailoring of human beings. While we may or may not consider linguistics to be a science in the strictest sense of the word, these "gadgets" can only be the results of discoveries in the "exact" sciences and their application. Thus, a large portion of science fiction includes such "gadgets" which involve advances in the sciences and could be said to qualify as science fiction in this way.

To say that science fiction is distinguished from other forms of fiction by the presence of some kind of science or derives its impetus from the sciences does not explain what fictional use is made of these materials. Whatever else may be said about this matter, it is certainly true that the "science" one finds in science fiction is not the same kind of "science" one finds in a textbook. An examination of an award-winning novel should help to clarify the roles which scientific materials can play in fiction. As mentioned earlier, *Babel-17* derives its major impetus from linguistics. More specifically, it is built around the reasonably well-established premise that different languages allow/force their users to view, and act on, the world in different ways. The book is *not* an explanation of why or how this is true. It is also built around the fact that we have developed several computer languages that are analytical and have elements which mean different things in different contexts. The book is *not* an explanation of computer languages and how they work. In fact, the basic story-line is a rather standard adventure story in which the hero sets out toward a goal, undergoes a series of tests, and emerges with greater power, as well as with the princess. What Delany has done with these premises is to postulate that an artificial, computer-like language has been developed as a weapon of sabotage and war. This postulate in turn informs the specific sequence of events and the specific ways in which they are carried out. Given the initial postulate, the setting must basically be a society involved in a war that has continued for some time and will include at least one specific setting that will be the object of sabotage; this is the setting of *Babel-17*.

Given this postulate, then, the story could go one of two ways: it could follow either the development and application of the language by one side against the other or follow the attempts of the side against whom it is being used to try to find out what it is, how it works, and how to counteract it. *Babel-17* chooses this latter course, which allows for more action and more attention to surrounding social conditions. This story-line, plus the initial postulate, requires that the main character be versed in linguistics, as well as have the typical virtues of the hero, and that the majority of the supporting characters be related to the war effort to helping the hero. These requirements are fulfilled in *Babel-17*, although with a twist, for the central character, Rydra Wong, is an extremely beautiful woman, a poetess with a talent for codes and languages. She has been married to a space captain, she is a novelist and is also a space captain; she also has many of the heroic virtues necessary for the role she must play. There are many other details surrounding these factors—the setting in the far future, inter-galactic civilization, the details of space flight and crew—but these are largely part of the background.

It is important to note that nowhere in this novel do we get a detailed description of the language; what we do get are indications of the major steps toward solving the puzzle and indications of the effects that the language has on the characters who speak it. For example, one of the major steps involves the discovery that the language has no words for "I" and "you"; we are shown this, and its effects, when Rydra tries to teach Butcher these concepts. Another demonstration of the nature and effects of the language is given when Rydra analyzes the room she is in and the supportive webbing restraining her, using this analysis to free herself. Thus, the scientific materials in this novel are not presented in their scientific form, but rather are converted to a process of discovery and to something which affects the life of particular human beings; the science involved is thus important only in its relations with people.

To summarize the discussion to this point: science fiction is a sub-genre of prose fiction which is distinguished from other kinds of fiction by the presence of an extrapolation of the human effects of an extrapolated science, broadly defined, as well as by the presence of "gadgets" produced by the technology resulting from extrapolated sciences. However, further modification of this definition is needed in order to cover adequately short stories and novels that are accepted as being science fiction.

Consider, for example, Roger Zelazny's novel *This Immortal*, which won the Hugo Award for 1966. In a very general sense, the underlying story-line is similar to that of *Babel-17*, with the hero embarking on a journey, undergoing a series of testing situations successfully, and, finally, achieving great power. Nevertheless, this is a very different novel, with an entirely different problem and an entirely different way of handling the presentation. The general setting is on Earth several hundred years after an atomic war has devastated the planet and made large areas uninhabitable; the radiation of that war has created many different kinds of mutations. The story also takes place after contact has been made with superior alien beings, so that a relatively small number of men remain on Earth, the rest of the survivors having chosen to emigrate and serve the aliens. These are the premises of the novel, with the first mentioned only briefly and mainly by indirection. Because the second premise is more closely related to the sequence of events, it is somewhat more prominent, seen throughout in some of the motivations of the characters. The story concerns Conrad Nomikos, a highly-placed Earth official, who is conducting an important Vegan on a tour of the Earth so that he may see what is left; during the course of this journey, he saves the life of the Vegan, as well as his own, a number of times, primarily from mutated beasts, although various men do have motives for killing him. Whereas many books would use a journey such as this as the springboard for a study of the psychology of the hero or of the sociology of a devastated world, *This Immortal* avoids such manipulation. It is true that these things are present, but they are not the main thrust of the book, nor do they seem particularly important, except perhaps as background. In fact, the closest thing to any central impact of "science" would seem to come either from mythology or historiography, depending on one's interpretation of the book. But even here, the postulate in either case influences the setting and the particular nature of what must be overcome rather than being used for the exploration of a scientific extrapolation. That is, mutation has produced a number of creatures that bear a resemblance to creatures in Greek mythology and Conrad, who is himself a mutant with characteristics similar to those of several mythic beings, embodies several concepts, such as the idea of fate, that are implicit in Greek myth and drama. But there is no attempt to follow closely any particular myth or group of myths or their effects. If this is an implied look at the difference between what actually happened and what history says happened, it is subordinate, only implied, and an adjunct to the process of testing Conrad in order to find out whether he should be granted great power.

However one chooses to interpret this novel, the definition of science fiction that we have developed so far, as well as most other definitions of the genre, often seems inadequate. But, in which ways does it qualify as science fiction and what are the implications these qualifications have for a definition of the field? First of all, there are many factors which place it within the genre: the facts that it takes place in the future after an atomic war, that mankind has made contact with alien intelligence, that the main character and other characters and creatures are mutations, that there is implied a means of space travel, all of these are commonly associated with science fiction. However, these do not seem to be enough, on their own merits, to classify the novel as science fiction, for these are at most side issues. What they have done, however, is to change, rather drastically, the conditions of life and environment which man must face. Into these conditions, Zelazny has put groups of characters, who face these altered conditions in a different manner. In creating this situation, Zelazny seems to be exploring the relationships between man and his world, not so much on a physical level as on an emotional, cultural, and mythic level. Among the questions that are explored in this novel, then, are: what is it that binds (some) men to Earth? what things from the past are worth preserving as conditions change? what things are necessary for survival on Earth under these changed conditions? what role will/should Earth play in the context of a galactic civilization? how will men react to all these changes? Although there are other issues that feed into this one, the question of the relationship between man and his world seems the most central and far-reaching. Thus, the field of science fiction includes a number of works which use the devices of science fiction to explore questions, ideas, and themes from a different perspective than that which is commonly available to us from other kinds of fiction and in our day-to-day lives.

It should also be noted that science fiction trappings are used for other purposes than those mentioned. There are those authors, for example, who include such things in an otherwise ordinary story in order to "dress it up" or, simply, to get it published. While these may be considered to be at least marginally science fiction, they cannot be considered good science fiction. There is also a fairly large number of novels and short stories commonly classified as "Sword and Sorcery." Many of these are straight adventure stories with strange and wondrous settings which add to the vicarious thrill of adventure, but have no other purpose. These authors substitute "wardles," for example, for horses, swords or other magic or primitive weapons for guns, and BEMs (Bug-Eyed Monsters) for Indians, but otherwise they use the same old "Cowboy and Indian" stories in new settings.

Not all "Sword and Sorcery" novels, however, are straight adventure and nothing more; many of the best of them explore the same sorts of topics that other kinds of science fiction deal with. "Space Opera" is related to War stories or Cowboy stories, and contains a high proportion of straight adventure, but it is the vehicle for a serious exploration of a variety of topics. One example of such stories is Isaac Asimov's Lucky Starr series; each story is adventure, with heroes and sidekicks and villains, and has a happy ending in which the hero flies his spaceship into the sunset. Nevertheless, reading any or all of these, the reader comes away with a great deal of information about the settings (various planets and asteroids in our solar system) and about the theory of space travel, which was valid at the time the stories were written. That a great deal of new information has rendered much of this information obsolete does not destroy the fact that anyone reading these stories (when they appeared) learned a great deal of current scientific theory, in addition to enjoying the adventures of Lucky Starr.

When we consider Arthur C. Clarke's *2001: A Space Odyssey*, we can observe several other aspects of science fiction. First of all, science fiction is not simply confined to projections into the future, for his subject is the evolutionary sweep of mankind from sub-human to human to something more-than-human, the Starchild. In order to show this sweep, the first part of the novel (and the movie) is necessarily set in the distant past. There is also a fairly sizable number of science fiction novels and short stories that are set in what might be called alternative-pasts and alternative-presents. For the most part, such stories explore the consequences of an historical event—if it had turned out differently. One such example explores the question "What would our world be like if the Spanish Armada had defeated the English fleet?" Another explores the consequences of a German victory in World War II. Still another postulates a victory for the South in the Civil War. (Of course, indirectly such novels explore the effects that these events have had on our lives.) The possibilities are enormous for such stories, although they remain a very small portion of published science fiction. Another feature of 2001 is its postulating explanations for events that have happened for which we have no explanation. That is, Clarke postulates a superior race that uses an incredible technology to assist the development of intelligent species by giving them boosts at the proper time in their development. We simply have no evidence that would explain why man made the leap from pre-human to human; similarly, we have no way of forecasting when, whether, how, and why man might make a leap from human to more-than-human. There are also other novels and short stories which have explored these questions, though few if any have the range covered in 2001.

Some novels and stories, however, do postulate explanations for unexplained phenomena. At least one deals with the fact that works of genius seem to tend to come in clusters, from men in the same place at the same time. At least one other postulates an explanation for what the writer sees as a trend toward pessimism in the last century or so. There are others which "explain" flying saucers; these range from the sober and serious to the absurd. Even though some of the explanations or postulated reasons for certain phenomena are rather esoteric, this sort of speculation has a legitimate place within the realm of science fiction.

Returning to *2001*, note that at least a part of the "science" in the novel is imaginary. The huge monoliths which guide man in his evolutionary path seem obviously to be some kind of communications equipment developed by a race with an extremely advanced technology. The sequence which takes the hero through life to death and rebirth as the Starchild is also induced by some scientific-technological means. Both of these things are not extrapolations from current science; they are what Clarke imagines the technology of a highly advanced race might be able to do. The computer aboard the ship is, of course, based on current computer technology; however, a quantum leap from both current psychological and computer knowledge seems necessary before a sentient computer can be developed, so that this, too, borders on the imaginary rather than the extrapolated. The means of space travel in this novel, however, seems to be an extrapolation, using current knowledge and theory. Imaginary science plays a very important role in science fiction, with the number of novels and short stories based on some imaginary science probably considerably outnumbering those based on straight extrapolation of current science. This is not necessarily a bad or negative sort of thing, but it does affect any definition of science fiction that might be developed.

At the last point of summary, our developing definition of science fiction read: "Science fiction is a sub-genre of prose fiction which is distinguished from other kinds of fiction by the presence of an extrapolation of the human effects of an extrapolated science, broadly defined, as well as by the presence of 'gadgets' produced by the technology resulting from extrapolated science."

Thus from the examples, many things that have been shown about science fiction: meetings with alien intelligences, mutation, advanced space travel, and future settings are all associated with science fiction; although the majority of science fiction stories are set in the future, the past and the present are also possible settings, especially when they present alternatives to the historical past and present. Whatever the setting, science fiction may be used to advance speculative explanations for actual events or trends for which we have no solid explanation. Writers may also use the format and devices of science fiction to explore themes that are not easily explored in other literary forms or to "teach" scientific facts and theories which are current at the time the story is written. The conditions of life and the environment that man must face are changed almost always in science fiction. The science in science fiction may be imaginary, as well as extrapolated current science; conventional story-lines seem the rule rather than the exception in science fiction; and the body of science fiction contains many bad stories, but these should not be the basis of judging the field. Although it might seem that an over-all definition resulting from these points would be extremely complex, it need not be, for there are several constants which run throughout these points and through the stories that have been examined.

One of the most important of these constants is that science fiction is concerned with the effects of change on human beings; this change may be brought about by the straight extrapolation of current scientific knowledge to its logical development in the near future. It may be caused by new factors that are related in some way to current science although we cannot logically predict them at this time; we can, in other words, speculate about future developments in the sciences. Or it may be caused by simply postulating the introduction of a set of factors which are not related to current science, such as the laws of magic or a change in a single detail of the past. Whatever brings about a change in the conditions of life, of environment, or of mind, science fiction is primarily concerned with examining the human effects of that change.

A second constant, which is basic to both science and science fiction, is the assumption that we live in an orderly universe. This idea is important since it means that the causes of the changed conditions can be discovered and explained and that the results will be regular and, within limits, predictable. For example, in *Babel-17*, the situation may seem chaotic, but the specific force of change in the novel, the language, has a structure and a logic which allows Rydra Wong to apply the laws and forms of linguistics both logically and intuitively in order to learn the language; furthermore, once she has learned it, she can change it with predictable results. *This Immortal* may seem less likely to observe this constant than many books considered science fiction; however, it is clear that Conrad believes that his action (or inaction) will have a definite effect on the course of human affairs. He also feels the need to find as much information as he can before he forms a hypothesis that will lead to action. Given the two premises of the book, the changed conditions are a logical result. Finally, even though the predictions that his son makes for him are not scientific, they do assume an order in the universe and they do accurately forecast the future; the problem with his son's prediction is not accuracy of prediction but rather accuracy of interpretation. There are many ways in which this constant can be demonstrated in the fiction, but it is necessary that it be present before a work can be considered science fiction.

Finally, one should note that in science fiction these two constants are normally balanced; that is, approximately equal emphasis is given to them in the development of the story. The explanation of the change, and of its causes and results, is at least as important to science fiction as the change itself. It can safely be said that the less these two constants are in balance, the less likely the work embodying them is to be science fiction.

It should be rather obvious by now that these points can be approached and handled in a variety of ways. For this reason, it is sometimes helpful to sub-divide the field of science fiction into smaller units based on the particular emphasis and approach to the constants.

A Way of Reading Science Fiction:
Another Look at *Dune*

Basically, there are six factors which compose a literary work, six things which can be separated rather easily for analysis: character, story, plot, narrative point-of-view, setting, and language. Together these not only provide the materials for the relationships that make up the book, they also work together to create the theme, the complex of meanings that interpret experience for us. Probably the first aspect of the work that needs attention in a thoughtful examination of a work of fiction is the story, the chronological-causal sequence of events. Although even this can become very complicated, what we are interested in here is the basic skeleton that holds all the rest of these elements together. For such purposes, a story event can be defined as a point at which the story makes a choice of directions, chooses one possibility rather than another. In written form, this would look rather like a list of events, or perhaps like an outline. Frank Herbert's *Dune*, one of three novels to win both the Hugo and the Nebula Awards, can provide an excellent example of how this approach works.

In spite of the length of the book, the basic story-line of *Dune* is quite simple. One way of summarizing that story would be the following sequence:

1. The Atreides family moves from Caladan to Arrakis.
2. The Harkonnens attack their stronghold, killing Duke Leto.
3. Paul and Lady Jessica escape into the desert.
4. They are captured by a group of Fremen.
5. Paul fights with and kills Jamis; as a result, he is accepted into the group.
6. Jessica becomes the Fremen's Reverend Mother.
7. Paul rides a sandworm, thus becoming fully initiated into the group.
8. Paul takes leadership of the Fremen.
9. The Fremen, under Paul, fight and defeat the Imperial forces.
10. Paul fights and kills Feyd-Rautha Harkonnen in formal duel.
11. Paul deposes the Emperor.

Each of these marks a point at which the story could go one of several directions, and each of them follows logically from, is "caused" by, what has gone before. It might be noted, too, that these also summarize a large number of specific actions. Furthermore, different people may very well add different elements to this list, or phrase them differently, for in part at least this is a matter of the point-of-view from which the actions of the book are seen; the reasoning behind the choices is as important as the choices themselves. Finally, more specific story events link each of these major events; for example, under Number 3 (Paul and Jessica escape into the desert), one would have such specific actions, in sequence, as their initial capture, being taken to the desert to be left helpless, escaping their guards, welcoming help from a group of Fremen led by Liet-Kynes, fleeing in an ornithopter through a desert storm, and walking across the desert. These specific steps lead from Number 3 directly to Number 4 on the above list. However, even without considering these specific steps or the details of the Harkonnen plotting which moves beside this story-line, this outline can suggest several things about the thematic content of the novel. First of all, these events show Paul's rise from the son of a murdered duke to the ruler of the Empire; certainly the political maneuvering involved in the novel will yield materials for a theme. At the same time that this rise is taking place, Paul also moves from a familiar place to a strange one, learns the ways of the strange situation, gradually becomes a member of a new group, and finally becomes a leader of that group; thematically, this suggests two directions: the learning process and the nature of the group he is becoming a part of.

In this novel, the next aspect that might be looked at is character, those qualities and traits that individuals in the novel are composed of, and at the relationships between characters. Paul's characteristics are many and varied, for comparatively speaking he is quite well-rounded. He has exceptional powers of observation and bodily control, having been trained in the Bene Gesserit way. His powers of logic and deduction are above normal, having been trained as a Mentat. He has a keen sense of the uses and intricacies of power and political maneuvering, having been raised as a duke's son who will one day take over his father's position. He is intelligent and is thus able to use these different kinds of training well. He has a gift of foretelling. He develops into the Kwisatz Haderach because of his genetic heritage, the necessities of life on Arrakis, the pressure of revenge for his father, and his training. Revenge is a strong motivating factor in many of his actions, particularly those dealing with the Emperor and the Harkonnens. He is also capable of love, though not for many people; he is loyal to those who look to him for leadership. Paul also has many other traits, and many relationships with other characters in the novel. There are many other characters, and the entire web of relationships is immense and complex. Those characteristics which have been indicated, however, can serve to show how story and character interact to clarify a thematic position.

One of the thematic areas suggested by the storyline is the learning process that Paul undergoes; the specifics of his character indicate the nature, the direction, and some of the means to achieve this learning. In the novel itself we are shown some of Paul's training in weapons, in thinking, in the use of physical control, and in practical government; for the most part, however, this kind of training is in the background, something that has already taken place. Instead, in the interaction between the events and his character, we see Paul gradually learning how to bring these various skills together, to understand their nature so that he can apply them to the specific problem of revenging his father and leading the Fremen to a position where they can safely work toward their goal of a green planet. As he learns to control these abilities, he also comes to understand more about himself and his place in his specific situation and in history. To a certain extent, his survival makes it necessary for him to learn these things, so that the setting will also be important to the learning process. Paul's abilities, plus his interaction with the Fremen and with the setting, as well as the desire for revenge, all coalesce to provide the means by which he finds the resources for growth. Through the course of the novel, he grows in several directions: in understanding himself, in his ability to control desired ends, in his ability to lead others, in his knowledge of the world around him, and in his ability to see himself as part of a much larger context. All of these things furnish further details for a thematic statement dealing with the learning process Paul undergoes. Other aspects of his character and of his relationships with other characters add depth, breadth, and detail to other thematic possibilities.

In many novels, the setting is simply where the action takes place, having minimal effect and minimal importance; in *Dune*, setting is one of the more important elements. In the largest sense, the setting is a distant galaxy, far in the future, which had originally been settled from Earth; a large number of planets are habitable and have been settled. Given the fact that there is an overall government for this system of inhabited planets, the physical facts of the distances and the size of the major political sub-divisions, the setting has an effect on the governmental system; although it does not demand a monarchy, a monarchy is a logical response to such conditions. The specific setting, the planet Arrakis, or Dune, affects most of the actions and is at least related to many of the character traits in the novel. Arrakis is a desert planet, with only a small supply of water, which is mostly concentrated in very tiny polar caps; its one point of importance for the governmental system is the fact that it alone produces melange, a spice which has many unique properties that make it valuable. Control of this spice, then, is a valuable thing, one which can lead to political maneuvering. However, it is the harshness of the planet that has the most wide-spread effect. In order to survive on such a planet, the Fremen must adapt nearly every facet of their existence to the facts of the planet, and so must most of those whose stay is only temporary. The lack of water, for example, requires that special clothing be worn to reclaim and recycle any traces of body moisture; it also conditions the society to reclaiming the body water of the dead before burial, and it gives rise to a variety of means for trapping and holding water in the air. The sand, the heat, and the giant sandworms all require adherence to a particular pattern of living. Quite naturally, these factors also condition the ceremonies, the attitudes, and the social customs of the people.

The battle for survival is intense; it does not take much urging from Leit-Kynes for the vision of Arrakis as a green planet to become both an obsession and a religious vision for the Fremen. This setting forces Paul to bend his powers toward survival; it provides a situation where learning to use the abilities that he has is imperative, whereas Caladan, his home planet, would have offered no challenge such as this. In order to rise, or even to be accepted, among these people, he must learn the ways of the desert, for if he does not, he can achieve none of his goals. The toughness required to survive is one of the factors in the defeat of the forces of the Emperor; another is that the Emperor's forces do not know the precautions that must be taken against the worms. More than these things, however, the setting and the attitudes of the various groups create what is one of the major themes of the novel, what might be called an ecological theme. There is a conflict between husbandry and exploitation, and between adapting to the land and adapting it to oneself. The answer provided is not simple: it suggests that something of both positions can be taken, if the ecology of the planet as a whole, including the people who live there, is taken into account before any changes are made or any use can be made of the resources. This point has bearing on many other aspects of the book: it conditions the political battles that are fought, it is a part of the learning process Paul undergoes, and it is a part of the religious element of the Fremen life. In this novel, then, the setting is important both in its own right and in its conditioning of the other elements of the novel.

The narrative point of view of *Dune*, on the other hand, is not likely to yield a great deal or to modify what is learned from other sources to any great extent. The narrator here is omniscient and seems to be objective in his presentation of the actions, the characters, and the setting. The reader gets much more emotional guidance through the language that is used to describe the characters and the situations. Two examples may suffice. One of these concerns the Baron Vladimir Harkonnen. We are never told directly that the Baron is villainous, but we know that he is. In the first place, his name is harsh sounding. When we are told that he uses suspensors to hold his body up, this image of gross fatness is repulsive. He speaks lovingly about the young boys that he will spend the night with (one of his reasons for going after the House of Atreides seems to be a passion for Paul). It is the way he speaks of his plans, even more than the plans themselves, that make him seem so underhanded and almost evil. Thus, the words which are used to describe him may seem neutral, but the imagery behind them guides the reader's emotional reaction so that our impression is negative.

Another example occurs during the night that Paul and Jessica spend in the stilltent just after they have escaped from the Baron's forces. Apparently they are waiting so that they can refresh themselves for the flight the next day. However, the things that happen in that tent, and the way in which they are described indicate that this is a significant experience for Paul. Note that before this event and continuing through the time they enter the tent, Paul has been following Jessica's lead; when they exit the next morning, Jessica is clearly aware that she is now following her son. The fact that at the beginning of the night Paul is unable to weep for his father, but is able to do so by the night's end, after he has come to grips with a number of things, is also significant; he is now able to react with understanding rather than confusion. Finally, much of the imagery of this section involves the womb and birth, so that Paul's emergence from the tent becomes a rebirth after returning to the depths of himself, to the womb, in order to find the resources he will need to cope with the situations he knows he must face. Although it is something that most people don't care to do, and although it is possible to get bogged down in the analysis of the language that is used to describe the various elements in a novel, some attention to such details is necessary if the fullest possible meaning and enjoyment are to be gained from a novel.

Character, setting, narrative point-of-view, and language are all aspects of plot; the major aspect of plot which has not been covered is the way in which the events and situations of the novel are presented.

In *Dune* the order of presentation is not a major factor, although the fact that we see much of what happens from both the Atreides and the Harkonnen sides of the question adds to our knowledge of the general situation and to the depth of many of the themes that are present in the novel. Nevertheless, the main interest in the way that these sections are put together is more technical than thematic and can be passed over quite lightly here; in other novels, however, the question of why the author arranged the events, or the telling of the events, in the order that he did may very well be worth a good deal of time and thought. (Joseph Conrad's *Lord Jim* is a novel in which the order of presentation has a great deal to do with its themes; one must understand this in order to appreciate the novel.)

Although the ways in which the various elements involved in the novel contribute to the formation of theme has been suggested in only one area, and a few other possible themes mentioned along the way, *Dune* is thematically rich and complex. In the case of each area of thematic concern, several of these elements contribute materials from which to build the theme and with which to modify it. It is not possible here to go into full detail about any single theme, much less to cover all of them adequately or to bring the many specific themes into a single statement of theme. A number of the general areas into which themes in this novel fall, however, can be suggested, along with some of the more specific possibilities. Thus, under the general heading of political themes, we find that the nature of power and its effects on those who have it or want it, the nature of true leadership, the functions of a system of checks and balances, and the relationships between vision and effective political voice are among the specific thematic topics dealt with. Under ecological themes, we find such topics as how a desert planet might be gradually made green in an ecologically sound way, adaptation to an environment, the social effects of an ecological system, and the necessity for political power if a system is to be changed. Under the general heading of psychological themes, we find an exploration of the maturation process, an examination of the effects of an unusual talent, a study of the stages by which an individual becomes a member of an alien group, a look at the ways in which an individual finds the inner resources necessary to meet the situations which face him, and a view of the effects of bitterness on a person's approach to his problems. There are also the religious themes: the coming of a prophesied messiah and of the ways in which men are blind to the purposes and workings of a higher principle even when they think they have control of their actions and purposes. These seem to cover most of the main factors in the novel, although there are other, lesser thematic elements, such as the love interest or the literary pretensions of the Princess Irulan. All of these points that have been mentioned concern at least two, and usually more, facets of the novel. This, plus the fact that the web of relationships between these points is very complex, makes it difficult to be satisfied with any single statement of theme. Nevertheless, the more precisely such a statement summarizes the basic point, and the more relationships with other points that it includes, the more adequate a summation of one of the thematic possibilities of the novel becomes.

When dealing with science fiction, there are several other points that can be profitably examined, whether before or after the sort of analysis suggested above.

Since many, though not all, science fiction stories and novels seem to have begun with the writer's speculation about what would happen if . . . , it is reasonable to try to determine what the core question of the work might be. That is, what question seems to give rise to the largest number of the specific factors in the novel? In the case of *Dune,* this core question seems to be something like this: what would happen if one had a desert planet that contained a valuable natural resource? The fact that it had a valuable resource would account for the interest in it and probably also for the fact that it is inhabited. The fact that it is a desert would account for the native social structure, the planet's ecology, and the difficulties posed for those who would exploit the resources. The properties of the spice account for its value to a divergent group of customers; that value in turn gives impetus to exploitation and the political maneuvering that accompanies the desire to gain the profits. As mentioned before, the political system found in the novel is at least one logical answer to this situation. Since a desert planet is not generally habitable, and cannot directly support more than a very few people, the existence of other settled planets is reasonable. If there are other planets, and travel between them, it is to be expected that the natives of Arrakis would have heard of green worlds, and that they would be taken by an ideal that is the opposite of their everyday existence, especially if there were someone to show the way. To have a hope of achieving that goal, an unusual political leader is necessary; the specific things which would make him unusual would not be specified by this requirement, but Paul certainly fits the bill. It may be true that not everything can be tied, directly or indirectly, back to this core question, but as it is stated it does provide a way of getting into an extremely large number of specific aspects of the novel; the points that have been mentioned are only the beginning. The main benefit of the core question is that it provides something quite specific to center one's thinking and discussion around, a point to which one can return and to which one can relate other points. It may also indicate themes or areas that one might be interested in speculating about. More than anything, though, it can provide a starting point for examining the work and a direction from which to work; it is especially valuable for science fiction because of the speculative nature of the field.

It also seems worthwhile to ask of any work just what it is that makes it science fiction. There may be no really solid answers to such a question, and for many books the answers will be rather superficial and not mean much. Nevertheless, there seem to be two basic types of answers to a question like this, which will indicate something about what the work is trying to do. One answer involves the core question, for in only a relatively small number of works is the core question a major factor in labeling the work as science fiction. If, for example, one asks the question: what might be the effects of a truly alien logical system, a question has been posed that can only be dealt with through science fiction. If, on the other hand, one asks such a question as "what might cause political revolution on the Moon?," the only thing about that question that might suggest science fiction is the fact that it sets the problem on the Moon. This is simply not the same kind of question, though the story based on one may be just as good as another. The second kind of answer to such a question, then, is that it is the devices or the setting or the characters, more than the basic impetus, which is responsible for categorizing a work as science fiction. There are two possibilities that one can choose between as to why the writer chose to use these science fiction elements: he did so in order to tell a familiar story in an unusual way, or whatever he wishes to explore is more easily, more clearly, or more purely explored if it need not be compared directly against historical reality. Much of science fiction seems to fall into this second category; it allows for the exploration of an alternative to current thought and action. The first possibility for this second answer usually yields some sort of adventure story; there is value in this kind of story, although it is the least likely of the possibilities to have more than momentary interest. Whichever one decides about an author's motivation for any given book, that choice will help to determine the direction of one's explanation of the work's purpose and significance and should help to develop an understanding of what science fiction is and does.

It is frequently suggested, often by those who would rather not spend the effort to do a good job of analysis, that analyzing a book takes all the enjoyment out of it. This may be true *if* the analysis is done for its own sake. However, if one has enjoyed a book, then analysis can help one understand more fully what one has enjoyed and why one enjoyed it. Perhaps the best argument for the idea that analysis provides greater enjoyment, however, is the science fiction fans themselves. Very few of them are trained literary scholars, but more than any other group of readers, they enjoy discussing the things that they have read. Not only that, but most of their arguments reveal that they have read carefully, thought about what they have read, and developed a keen sense of the patterns and the relationships in what they have read. The gusto with which they argue their points derived from this careful, intelligent, thoughtful reading and later cogitation suggests that their enjoyment has been enhanced, rather than destroyed, by the process. It does take some time getting used to thinking carefully and seriously about any kind of literary form, but ultimately the reward—a more complete experience of the work—is worth the effort.

Guidelines for Reading
Science Fiction

The following questions can be used as a guideline for thinking about any literary work, although questions 9 and 12 through 15 apply specifically to science fiction. It is not particularly recommended that each question be answered fully for each novel or story; for any particular story, some questions are more relevant than others. Their main benefit is in focusing attention on specific aspects of something one has read, in order to help develop materials leading to a more complete understanding.

1. What are the major story-events in the work?
2. Who are the major characters in the work and what are their major characteristics?
3. What seem to be the major relationships between characters and between groups of characters?
4. What functions do these characters serve in the chronological-causal sequence of events? in the work as a whole?
5. What are the major details of the physical setting of the novel?

6. How does this setting affect other aspects of the work?

7. What are the major details of the social setting of the work?

8. How does the social setting affect other aspects of the work?

9. What do you consider to be the motivating core of the work? That is, what question or concept seems to have given impetus to the work?

10. What themes do you think are present in the work? What details would support your ideas?

11. What is the narrative point-of-view in the work? That is, who is telling the story, where is he in relation to the action, and what attitudes does he exhibit in telling the story?

12. What makes this work science fiction?

13. What purposes do the science fiction elements serve in the work?

14. Could this work have been written as non-science fiction?

15. What is gained (or lost) through the use of science fiction elements?

On Verisimilitude and the Suspension of Disbelief in Science Fiction

Although the surface meanings of these two terms would seem to cast them as opposites, they are actually very close companions in approaching *any* literary form—science fiction, "mainstream" fiction, poetry or drama. Basically, verisimilitude can be defined as the quality of appearing to be true or real or likely. The suspension of disbelief refers to the act of deferring or postponing one's judgment about the truth, reality, or likelihood of something, in this case a literary work or some aspect of it. When a person reads any literary work, he comes to it knowing that in a literal, factual, or historical sense the work is not true; that is, he knows that the events and characters presented did not happen or do not exist as described. Furthermore, most readers expect that the literary work will present an interpretation of human experience that will have broader reverberations and applications beyond the confines of the particular events and characters of the work. *Because* of this knowledge and these expectations, the reader, before he ever begins the work, provisionally suspends his disbelief; although it is rarely verbalized, the underlying thought runs something like this: "Okay, so I know this isn't literally true. But this work may provide a different perspective on things that I didn't have before, or it may suggest a way of acting and reacting to things that I hadn't considered before. Therefore, I will accept the author's premises and let him try to convince me that he has the measure of reality, a valid interpretation of experience, in this work."

This suspension of disbelief initially allows the writer the opportunity to gradually build a sense of verisimilitude—a sense of being true or real. However, it is also something that the reader carries with him throughout his reading of the work, for at no time is he likely to become convinced suddenly that this *is* real or factual—only that it is lifelike or possible or that it illuminates some aspect of reality. The creation of a sense of verisimilitude must begin early in the work, with its heaviest concentration in the first chapter or two, but the effort must continue throughout the book, consistent with what has gone before; if the writer does not make this effort, then even the most willing suspension of disbelief will disappear and the work will be rejected.

Both of these points are important for any literary work, and sometimes they are difficult to achieve. This is doubly true for science fiction, for in many people there is a reluctance to set aside, even provisionally, their disbelief when presented with a futuristic setting or with an alternative to things as we know them now; there is also a reluctance to accept in these circumstances the devices which would create a sense of verisimilitude in a novel or short story set in the present or in the past. In addition, when the reader is moved into a situation with which he is almost totally unfamiliar, more attention to details, to

245

the creation of an entire world, is needed than if the situation were somewhat similar to his situation. Finally, the reader's sense of verisimilitude will be slightly different when he encounters science fiction than with so-called mainstream fiction; that is, instead of feeling that it could be real or likely to be real, he will feel that it is possible or likely to be possible. A bad writer in any field will fail to create a sense of verisimilitude to some degree, and this applies to science fiction; but it is probably more apparent in science fiction because the writer is not working with a familiar situation and where the reader cannot, automatically, supply details which the writer has left out. Once again, however, to say that there is bad science fiction or science fiction which is not well written is *not* to condemn the entire field; science fiction, like anything else, should be judged by its best examples, not its worst.

There seems to be no way of arguing someone into suspending his disbelief, but there are several factors that help to induce a suspension of disbelief. The more literature a person has read, the easier it is for him to suspend his disbelief and to accept the sense of verisimilitude, for he is more aware—consciously or unconsciously—of the conventions of the genre he is reading. Thus, a person who has read a great deal of fiction that is not science fiction seems to have an easier time moving into science fiction and accepting it than someone who has read very little fiction of any kind. And, of course, someone who has read a great deal of science fiction finds it easier to suspend disbelief and to pick up the clues which create verisimilitude than someone who has read a great deal of other kinds of fiction, again because of a firmer sense of what to expect and because of a familiarity with the conventions. Another factor involved in the initial suspension of disbelief is interest. There is, of course, no predicting what might strike a person's interest. However, a person who is interested in, say, languages might find Jack Vance's *The Languages of Pao* easier to accept than most other science fiction because his interest and the topic of the book coincide. It might be the illustration on the cover of the book that strikes his interest. It may be the recommendation of a friend. Whatever the specific thing that sparks the interest, the coinciding of personal interest and an aspect of the book will make acceptance much easier and will make any resistance to science fiction less difficult to overcome. A third factor is knowledge. In a rather general sense, the more that a person knows about anything, the more likely he will be to realize that multiple ways of looking at things are normal and right, that there is no one right answer to any question; this, of course, is a perfect way to read science fiction, which takes familiar elements into an unfamiliar situation in order to test the outcome. Or to put it another way, science fiction sets the conditions for the perception of some aspect of reality and allows the interaction of the elements (story, character, etc.) within these guidelines; the more aware a person is that the mode of perception determines what can be seen, the more likely he is to enjoy science fiction. On a more specific plane, this is also true. That is, the more a reader knows about what to expect in science fiction, the more easily he can respond to it. Thus, knowing about some of the conventions of the sub-genre, about some of the assumptions that are made, about some of the typical procedures involved, and about some of the purposes of science fiction can be very helpful in facilitating the suspension of disbelief. These things, fortunately, can be taught or learned. What it finally comes down to is this: the open-minded reader is the person who is most willing to suspend his disbelief, allow the writer his premises, and give the writer a chance to show that his work has a bearing on life, reality, or experience. This attitude can be fostered and guided, but it cannot be forced.

Once the reader has suspended his disbelief, however tentatively or provisionally, the writer's responsibility begins. There are a number of devices and methods he can use, some of which are applicable to all of fiction and others of which are peculiar to science fiction. One device that may be used when the subject matter is such that the reader can be expected to be skeptical is to use a central viewpoint character who is himself skeptical initially but who gradually becomes convinced. If the character is drawn well enough so that the reader can identify with him at all, the reader will be drawn along the same path taken by the character, though perhaps not as far. Harold Shea in *The Incomplete Enchanter*, by L. Sprague de Camp and Fletcher Pratt, is a good example of this; in fact, this book uses many of the devices available to the writer who would create verisimilitude effectively. Harold Shea is a young experimental psychologist who is part of a team with an institutional grant; he is dissatisfied with the life he is living and has a hankering for a more adventurous life. It is important that he is a psychologist, for this gives him an analytical approach to things and suggests that he is not likely to be fooled by people or by himself; the reader is given several examples of these traits before anything unusual begins.

When Harold Shea is thrust into an unknown world,

he is careful to note the conditions in which he finds himself, comparing them with his expectations. He does not accept what he is told readily—he is suspicious, he is cautious, he is skeptical, and he is analytical. In a number of instances, he lists the possibilities that might explain what has happened to him; he chooses the explanation that most of us would choose, *then* he throws out the one bit of evidence that doesn't fit that explanation but rather points toward the explanation the reader should accept. Even when he becomes more or less convinced that he is in a world where the laws of magic work, he views his first attempts at applying these laws as fakery and mumbo-jumbo; he is extremely surprised when it works. In this case, the reader is drawn into acceptance of the possibility that this might happen because, among other things, the character with whom he identifies follows a step-by-step process from skepticism to belief. Of course, not all novels use or need this kind of character and character change. In perhaps the majority of cases, the same function is served when the characters involved accept what seems to us strange as merely part of the normal process of living. Even in *The Incomplete Enchanter* this can be seen. First of all, in the world of gods and magic, there is a foil for Shea, a human inhabitant of that world who simply accepts the things that happen as the way things are supposed to happen. A second such character exists in Harold's (and our) normal world, Harold's boss, who listens to his story when he returns, observes the changes in Harold, and accepts the story. Thus, characters can act as an aid in creating a sense of verisimilitude or in urging the reader to continue in his suspension of disbelief.

Another method that is frequently used in science

fiction is an early explanation of the theoretical basis for the unusual situation; this is referred to, directly and indirectly, throughout the story. For example, in *The Incomplete Enchanter*, the theory of paraphysics, which postulates that attuning oneself to a different series of impressions will put one into a world where those impressions exist, is discussed in a cold, sober scientific setting for several pages of the first chapter. Another such discussion takes place near the middle of the novel, after Harold has returned from his first journey into another worldview. Between these two discussions, and during the second journey, a number of references are made to this theoretical base, particularly in connection with the practical applications of the theory. Another example, from quite a different novel, occurs in *The Moon Is a Harsh Mistress* when Mannie provides a theoretical base for a sentient computer. It happens that in both these cases the "science" which provides the theoretical base is imaginary, though in different ways. That is, there is a body of knowledge pertaining to magic and the occult, but whereas "paraphysics" draws on this body of knowledge, there is currently no science of magic, no paraphysics. With the sentient computer, on the other hand, the points made about the human mind and human psychology seem to be valid; however, there is no existing connection between human psychology and computer psychology, and hence no "real" basis for making the comparison that is made. Of course, not all scientific explanations in science fiction draw on imaginary science, but many of them do. It is important to remember that a theory, whether it be Einstein's or anyone else's, is not a fact; it is only a hypothetical explanation, based on certain assumptions, of a number of observed data. What is really important here is not the source of the theoretical explanation provided in the story but, instead, simply the fact that it is there, that an organized explanation can be formulated for the things that happen. It is all the better if this explanation can be drawn directly from existing scientific knowledge and theory, but when one is dealing with extrapolated science this is not often possible. Consequently, the mere presence of a theoretical explanation, particuarly in concert with other elements working toward the creation of a sense of verisimilitude, helps to make an unfamiliar situation or series of actions more believable or acceptable.

A third means for creating verisimilitude, which perhaps has the most currency of all, is the construction of a solid portrait of the situation and setting involved through the use of details. Because such details must be very specific and included throughout the novel at appropriate moments, good examples are somewhat difficult to provide; the best thing to do would be to read any book, but especially science fiction, looking specifically for details which help one build a picture of the world of the story so that one is able to visualize it: these are details at work creating a sense of verisimilitude. Any situation or series of actions that one can picture in his mind is easier to accept and believe than those that he cannot picture. Some general examples of the sorts of details that might be used for this purpose should be helpful. The more unfamiliar a setting is, a proportionally greater amount of detail used to describe that setting will be needed to give it a sense of reality. In *The Incomplete Enchanter,* for instance, when the setting is in the Garaden Hospital, the setting is established by the name alone and most of the detail in that section of the novel is spent on establishing the characters, but when Harold lands in the world of Norse myth, the first six paragraphs deal almost totally with the setting in which he has landed, and much of the rest of Chapter 2 contains further information about the setting; in addition, whenever new features of setting are encountered, they too are described quite clearly. Details about where and how the inhabitants of an unfamiliar place live also add a feeling of reality to the situation. Thus, descriptions of the houses they live in, the kinds of furniture used, food eaten and clothing worn, the relationships between men and women—these, and many other similar details, help to build a more solid picture of a world that *could* be real.

Finally, details about the inhabitants themselves, about the way they think and talk and act, add to the believability of an unfamiliar setting and situation. If, for example, this setting is in the world of Norse mythology, as it is in *The Incomplete Enchanter*, it will be enhanced if one or more characters speak, on appropriate occasions, with quotations from what seems to be Eddic Poetry. Another example of this technique is to characterize the gods involved with the characteristics they are given in Norse myth, since many people have at least a fragmentary knowledge of these myths; of course, the characterization may go beyond this to meet the needs of the particular story being told, but this must be consistent with those established traits. Now, in order for this compiling of details of various kinds to be effective in persuading the reader to accept it as having some kind of reality or possibility, these details should form a consistent, coherent pattern. Any point of inconsistency which is not somehow explained will, or can, destroy the whole job that has been done; to do this takes very little: a single detail or a single utterance by even a minor character that is inconsistent is enough to bring the whole structure down in some cases, though some inconsistencies may be easier to accept and overlook than others. Consequently, although this structure of details which builds the portrait of a world is very important in creating a sense of verisimilitude, it is a fragile thing; the wonder is not that it sometimes fails, but rather that it works so often.

A fourth method that can be very helpful in making the reader feel more familiar with an unusual situation and setting is the use of a more or less standard story-line, although this can also rebound severely. That is, there seem to be three basic story-patterns that are used as the vehicle for a sizable portion of science fiction. The first of these is the adventure story where the hero journeys from a starting point to a goal, undergoing a series of adventures along the way. With one kind of emphasis, these can be used to show the development from child to adult; in science fiction, this process will be undertaken in a new society or with rules or situations unlike those we know, but the results and the story will be the same. With another kind of emphasis, these can show the process by which the hero finds within himself the resources needed to meet the tasks facing him. With still another kind of emphasis, the story-pattern can be used to explore a variety of facets of a culture unlike our own, or it can be used to demonstrate the phases or aspects of some hypothesis. It is not the story-pattern that is really important; rather, the emphasis and the details that are overlaid on this pattern determine the thrust and the interest of the novel.

Another frequently used pattern follows the progress of the scientific method: in an unusual situation, the hero gathers the facts available to him, formulates a theory for his situation, predicts the consequences of certain actions, and verifies his theories and predictions by acting on them. The situation in which the hero finds himself and the particular ideas which the author wishes to explore will, of course, determine the emphasis and interest of the novel, for this process itself can be applied to almost any subject matter imaginable. The third pattern which is present, though not often independently, is the how-to-do-it pattern, in which the hero takes the reader step-by-step through some process, which might be creating and carrying out a revolution or might be instructions on building and flying a rocketship—or any of a large number of other particular topics. Once again, with each of these basic patterns, the variety of ideas that can be explored and the differences in emphasis can be used to make the novels and short stories using them seem entirely different, which is as it should be. When we consider that these can be combined among themselves, or with other patterns, the possibilities of difference are further enhanced. The advantage gained through their use is that the writer can concentrate on exploring the situation and the idea, for the organization is quite rigid and can take care of itself; the reader can also give his attention to the situation and the idea, since he will not have to spend a great deal of time figuring out what is happening, and at the same time he will have an underlying feeling that there is something familiar about what is going on.

There is a general consensus that there are only a very few human stories to be told, though there may be many particular instances, emphases, and variations for those few. If, however, the basic pattern becomes too obtrusive or if the material overlaying it—the particular interests of the novel—are not developed fully and interestingly, then the reaction of most readers is likely to be scorn for the novel and the writer. But this reaction is likely to be true only if the reader is forced to become aware of this pattern while reading; becoming aware during later analysis does not seem to produce the same results. This is particularly true of the adventure pattern. Even so, while these patterns can, if done skillfully, add to the sense of verisimilitude for science fiction, they cannot do so alone; they must have the support and assistance of all the other methods available to the writer.

A fifth means that science fiction writers particularly use to avoid unbelievability is to keep the changes that the reader must accept to a minimum, maximizing familiar elements. This does not always mean that most things in the novel or short story will be familiar. It does mean, given the basic premises of the work, that everything in the work should be derived from those premises and be consistent with them, and that, whenever possible within that framework, familiar elements will be used. Most often the most strikingly familiar element will be in human nature. No matter what predicament the characters find themselves in, their actions and reactions and their thoughts and words will be recognizable to us as things we ourselves might do or think, or as things that are confirmed by our knowledge of other human beings. Even when the beings involved are alien in some way, they are characterized in human terms for the most part, with some difference to suggest their alienness. For example, in *The Incomplete En-*

chanter, once we accept the possibility of moving from one world (and worldview) to another, the things that Harold Shea does, the things that he feels, the things that he asks questions about, and so on, are things that most of us would do, feel, and say—or at least if we found ourselves in that situation. Furthermore, the characteristics which separate the Norse gods from men are very few: they are somewhat larger and stronger than Harold, but then so are the humans of the world; they have a piercing eye, which can freeze a man or measure him totally, but they rarely use this. Each of them seems to have some specialized talents, for Heimdall is sleepless and can see long distances, while Loki is a magician, but in other ways they are human, most needing sleep and so on; four of them have magical weapons, though these will serve man as well as god; and, of course, they are conscious, to varying degrees, of their responsibilities and place among men. But they drink, they fight and argue, they sleep (except Heimdall), they brag, they get into trouble that others must help them out of, and they do all the rest of the things mere mortals do, although on a slightly larger scale.

In Gordon R. Dickson's *None But Man*, the aliens are humanoid, though taller and thinner than man, and with different articulation of the joints; the main difference, however, is that their ethical-moral-social-political system is based on respectability rather than rightness, the reverse of our own. Of course, we have some understanding of at least some aspects of respectability, so we are not too disoriented, and once we accept that change in motivational base, the rest of their actions are consistent with it and recognizable in human terms. Even in a novel like James Blish's *A Case of Conscience*, where the aliens are intelligent dinosaur-like beings, they are characterized as purely rational beings; pure rationality has been postulated as an ideal condition for man, so that this characterization is based on an ideal of human nature. Of course, there are also novels and short stories where the aliens are characterized in terms of the worst human traits instead of the best. This constancy of human nature, or aspects of it, does a great deal to help the reader see the relevance of the more unusual elements in the work, as well as to concentrate his attention on those elements.

The other part of this fifth method is somewhat more difficult, for it still involves a great deal of the unusual. That is, even when you give the writer his premises, suspending your disbelief of them, the particulars that flow from these premises, especially in science fiction, are likely to seem extraordinary for most people. Nevertheless, if these particulars flow logically from the premises, a degree of verisimilitude is created. To use *The Incomplete Enchanter* as an example once again, there are just two premises that have to be accepted for the sake of the exploration (they are not accepted on faith, for some explanation is provided): that there are/were worlds in which the laws of magic operate and that it is possible to transfer into such worlds. Everything else follows from these premises—and follows logically. The second of these premises is largely a vehicle, a means of manipulating a character we can sympathize with into the world of magic so it can be explored. As far as the first premise is concerned, the world of Norse myth is a logical choice, since it is a world that believed in magic. It is also a world peopled by gods, trolls and giants, as well as by humans; consequently, it is logical and expected that these should appear in the novel and that they should have distinctive characteristics, with the gods portrayed the most favorably. The world of Norse myth is a cold and, in a sense, an unformed world. In connection with this, if we accept the idea of transfer between worlds, it seems reasonable that the fabric of any world is weakest and hence most likely to admit outside elements in times of crisis. In the world of Norse mythology, this time is Fimbulwinter, severe winter during the summer, and this is precisely where Harold finds himself. From these factors flow many of the details of the setting, the clothing, the action, and even the conversation. Furthermore, if this is a world where the laws of magic hold, then the laws of physics and chemistry are likely not to hold (although there are some stories that postulate that they can exist side by side); consequently, it is entirely logical that Harold's pistol and matches do not work. In fact, if either or both of those "imported" items did work, given the explanations early in the book, it would introduce an element that is inconsistent with the premises on which the story is built and would therefore destroy the illusion of reality that has been built through the logical structure of the details of a world built on these premises. Once again, the illusion of reality, the acceptance of possibility, is difficult to build; it is a fragile structure no stronger than its weakest member.

These five methods seem to be the most important of the means by which the writer, especially the science fiction writer, builds from the reader's willing suspension of disbelief to create an illusion of possibility. It is, of course, important that the reader be a party to this creation, remaining open to the suggestions made and willing to see the connections between the elements provided. In a very real sense, it is impossible to convince a reader of science fiction of the reality of what he is reading, but it may be possible to convince him of the possibility of what he is reading. Even so, science fiction, perhaps more than any other literary genre, depends on the reader's sense of intellectual play—that is, on his willingness to begin with the question "What would happen if . . . ?" or "What would it be like if . . . ?" and to follow the logical development of possible answers to an end. In this case, the writer must do all the things delineated above, and use any other devices available to him, to help the reader identify with the situation created and to feel that what he is reading is *a* logical, possible answer to the question posed. If he succeeds in doing at least this, then the writer of science fiction has succeeded in creating a sense of verisimilitude and has made the reader's willing suspension of disbelief worthwhile.

Awards for Science Fiction

There are two major awards given each year for high quality work in the field of science fiction, the Hugo and the Nebula.

More formally known as The Science Fiction Achievement Awards, the Hugo Awards are determined by the popular vote of science fiction readers attending the current year's World Science Fiction Convention. The more popular name, the Hugo, is due to Hugo Gernsback, one of the "fathers" of modern science fiction, as a writer, editor and publisher. The basic design of a Hugo is of a rocket ship poised for take-off above a block of wood, although design details and materials have varied from year to year. The categories for which Hugos have been awarded have also varied from year to year; in addition to the awards for fiction of various lengths, there have been awards for such categories as Best Fanzine (the insider's name for amateur publications related to science fiction), Best Fan Writer, Best Fan Artist, Best Professional Magazine, Best Professional Artist, Best Motion Picture, Best Dramatic Presentation, and a number of other such areas. These awards were first given in 1953 at the eleventh convention, held in

Philadelphia; they were not given in 1954, but were resumed the following year and have been awarded each year since then.

The Nebula Awards are presented each year by the Science Fiction Writers of America through a nominating and balloting process in which all the members participate; the actual awarding of these trophies, which are a spiral nebula of metallic glitter and a rock crystal specimen embedded in a block of lucite, is held each spring at simultaneous Nebula Awards Banquets held in New York, New Orleans and on the West Coast. The Science Fiction Writers of America was founded in 1965, and in the spring of 1966 awarded the first Nebulas. The categories for which they are awarded have remained stable since the beginning; they are: Best Novel, Best Novella, Best Novelette, and Best Short Story.

As might be expected, each of these awards has its particular slant. The Hugos seem to emphasize the qualities of interest and provocation of speculation somewhat more heavily, while the Nebulas seem to give slightly more emphasis to technical qualities such as the handling of characterization or plot and the development of an idea. This is, of course, as it should be, for readers and writers inevitably have different perspectives on the field. However, whichever award a work has gotten, it is most likely to be well worth reading if it has gotten either of the awards. It should be noted, though, that the quality of novels and shorter fiction which have received awards is not uniform, quite probably because of changing tastes and because of the works available to select from during any given year; some award-winning works have been forgotten within a few years of their publication. It seems to be true that the works of the highest quality,

261

both as fiction and as science fiction, are those which have won both of the awards. There are, however, some drawbacks to a statement of this sort because the main ones being the fact that both awards have been given for only eight years, and the fact that novels published before 1952, many of them very good, were not available for these awards. Nevertheless, such criteria can be used as a basis for finding good science fiction initially and using this as a basis for further judgment.

In the lists of award-winning fiction which follow, it should be noted that the dates given are the dates of publication; the awards in all cases were given the following year. It should also be noted that at the time of this writing, the Nebula Awards for works published in 1972 have been announced, but the Hugos had not. Finally, the Science Fiction Writers of America have chosen a number of works published before 1965 which they feel to be either of high quality or of historical interest, and are republishing them as *The Science Fiction Hall of Fame*. Volume I (short stories), edited by Robert Silverberg, and Volumes IIa and IIb (novellas and novelettes), edited by Ben Bova, are now available. In addition, the shorter (less than novel length) award-winning fiction is available. Isaac Asimov has edited *The Hugo Winners*, which includes all shorter fiction which has won the Hugo, in one hardbound volume; it will be in two volumes in paper, with the first volume already on the racks. Nebula Award stories are published annually, together with runners-up, under the general title *Nebula Award Stories;* the most recent is *Nebula Award Stories Seven*, edited by Lloyd Biggle, Jr., and includes the winners from 1971 (with the awards given in 1972). The lists that follow, then, as well as these other volumes, are excellent sources of good science fiction, with enough variety to please any taste.

AWARD-WINNING NOVELS

The Demolished Man, by Alfred Bester (1952, Hugo)

They'd Rather Be Right, by Mark Clifton and Frank Riley (1954, Hugo)

Double Star, by Robert A. Heinlein (1955, Hugo)

The Big Time, by Fritz Leiber (1957, Hugo)

A Case of Conscience, by James Blish (1958, Hugo)

Starship Troopers, by Robert A. Heinlein (1959, Hugo)

A Canticle for Leibowitz, by Walter M. Miller, Jr. (1960, Hugo)

Stranger in a Strange Land, by Robert A. Heinlein (1961, Hugo)

The Man in the High Castle, by Philip K. Dick (1962, Hugo)

Way Station, by Clifford Simak (1963, Hugo)

The Wanderer, by Fritz Leiber (1964, Hugo)

And Call Me Conrad, by Roger Zelazny (1965, Hugo) Now titled: *This Immortal.*

Dune, by Frank Herbert (1965, Hugo and Nebula)

The Foundation Trilogy, by Isaac Asimov (given a retroactive Hugo in 1966 as the best all-time series)

The Moon Is a Harsh Mistress, by Robert A. Heinlein (1966, Hugo)

Flowers for Algernon, by Daniel Keyes (1966, Nebula) The novel, not the short story.

Babel-17, by Samuel R. Delany (1966, Nebula)

Lord of Light, by Roger Zelazny (1967, Hugo)

The Einstein Intersection, by Samuel R. Delany
 (1967, Nebula)

Stand on Zanzibar, by John Brunner (1968, Hugo)

Rite of Passage, by Alexei Panshin (1968, Nebula)

The Left Hand of Darkness, by Ursula K. LeGuin
 (1969, Hugo and Nebula)

Ringworld, by Larry Niven (1970, Hugo and Nebula)

To Your Scattered Bodies Go, by Philip José Farmer
 (1971, Hugo)

A Time of Changes, by Robert Silverberg (1971,
 Nebula)

The Gods Themselves, by Isaac Asimov (1972, Hugo
 and Nebula)

AWARD-WINNING SHORTER FICTION

1952

No short fiction awards.

1954

"The Darfsteller," by Walter M. Miller, Jr. (novelette, Hugo)

"Allamagoosa," by Eric Frank Russel (short story,
Hugo)

1955

"Exploration Team," by Murray Leinster (novelette,
Hugo)

"The Star," by Arthur C. Clarke (short story, Hugo)

1956

No short fiction awards.

1957

"Or All the Seas with Oysters," by Avram Davidson (short story, Hugo)

1958

"The Big Front Yard," by Clifford Simak (novelette, Hugo)

"The Hell-Bound Train," by Robert Bloch (short story, Hugo)

1959

"Flowers for Algernon," by Daniel Keyes (short fiction, Hugo)

1960

"The Longest Voyage," by Poul Anderson (novelette, Hugo)

1961

The Hothouse series by Brian W. Aldiss (short fiction, Hugo)

1962

"The Dragon Masters," by Jack Vance (short fiction, Hugo)

1963

"No Truce With Kings," by Poul Anderson (short fiction, Hugo)

1964

"Soldier, Ask Not," by Gordon R. Dickson (short fiction, Hugo)

1965

" 'Repent, Harlequin!' said the Ticktockman," by Harlan Ellison (short fiction, Hugo; short story, Nebula)

"The Saliva Tree," by Brian W. Aldiss (novella, Nebula)

"He Who Shapes," by Roger Zelazny (novella, Nebula)

"The Doors of His Face, the Lamps of His Mouth," by Roger Zelazny (novelette, Nebula)

1966

"The Last Castle," by Jack Vance (novelette, Hugo; novella, Nebula)

"Call Him Lord," by Gordon R. Dickson (novelette, Nebula)

"The Secret Place," by Richard McKenna (short story, Nebula)

"Neutron Star," by Larry Niven (short story, Hugo)

1967

"Weyr Search," by Anne McCaffrey (novella, Hugo)

"Riders of the Purple Wage," by Philip José Farmer (novella, Hugo)

"Gonna Roll the Bones," by Fritz Leiber (novelette, Hugo and Nebula)

"I Have No Mouth, And I Must Scream," by Harlan Ellison (short story, Hugo)

"Behold the Man," by Michael Moorcock (novella, Nebula)

"Aye, and Gomorrah," by Samuel R. Delany (short story, Nebula)

1968

"Nightwings," by Robert Silverberg (novella, Hugo)

"The Sharing of Flesh," by Poul Anderson (novelette, Hugo)

"The Beast That Shouted Love at the Heart of the World," by Harlan Ellison (short story, Hugo)

"Dragonrider," by Anne McCaffrey (novella, Nebula)

"Mother to the World," by Richard Wilson (novelette, Nebula)

"The Planners," by Kate Wilhelm (short story, Nebula)

1969

"Ship of Shadows," by Fritz Leiber (novella, Hugo)

"Time Considered as a Helix of Semi-Previous Stones," by Samuel R. Delany (short story, Hugo; novelette, Nebula)

"A Boy and His Dog," by Harlan Ellison (novella, Nebula)

"Passengers," by Robert Silverberg (short story, Nebula)

1970

"Ill Met in Lankhmar," by Fritz Leiber (novella, Hugo and Nebula)

"Slow Sculpture," by Theodore Sturgeon (short story, Hugo; novelette, Nebula)

1971

"The Queen of Air and Darkness," by Poul Anderson (novella, Hugo; novelette, Nebula)

"Inconstant Moon," by Larry Niven (short story, Hugo)

"The Missing Man," by Katherine MacLean (novella, Nebula)

"Good News from the Vatican," by Robert Silverberg (short story, Nebula)

1972

"A Meeting With Medusa," by Arthur C. Clarke (novella, Nebula)

"Goat Song," by Poul Anderson (novelette, Nebula)

"When It Happened," by Joanna Russ (short story, Nebula)

AWARD-WINNING MAGAZINES

The following magazines have all won a Hugo Award as the Best Professional Magazine at least once.

Galaxy

Words of IF

New Worlds Science Fiction (British)

The Magazine of Fantasy and Science Fiction

Analog Science Fiction/Science Fact (This magazine has won the award both under its current title and under its former title of *Astounding Science Fiction*, all awards being won under the editorship of John W. Campbell.)

A Selected Bibliography of
Science Fiction

The list which follows makes no claim to being complete or of including all the science fiction that is historically interesting, that is worth rereading, or that is merely fun to read. A number of inveterate readers of science fiction have contributed to this listing; thus, someone who is acquainted with the field has found each of these items historically interesting, worth reading several times, or enjoyable—and in many cases, the items fit at least two, if not all three, of these criteria. This list is designed primarily to help you find good science fiction should you wish to explore the field further. It should be noted that most of these items are novels, and that fantasy and anthologies have not been given much attention, although there are some entries for each. Using this list as a starting point, add items of your own, according to your interests, as you come across them.

ALDISS, BRIAN

  Barefoot in the Head
  Galaxies like Grains of Sand
  The Long Afternoon of Earth

Neanderthal Planet
Starswarm

ANDERSON, POUL

The Byworlder
Brain Wave
The Corridors of Time
The Dancer From Atlantis
The Horn of Time
Operation Chaos
Shield
The Star Fox
Three Hearts and Three Lions
Un-Man
Virgin Planet

ANTHONY, PIERS

Macroscope
Omnivore
Orn
The Ring (with ROBERT MARGOFF)
Sos the Rope

ASIMOV, ISAAC

The Caves of Steel
The Currents of Space
The End of Eternity
Fantastic Voyage
The Foundation Trilogy
    Foundation
    Foundation and Empire
    Second Foundation
The Gods Themselves

I, Robot
Is Anybody There?
Lucky Starr and the Big Sun of Mercury
Lucky Starr and the Moons of Jupiter
Lucky Starr and the Oceans of Venus
Lucky Starr and the Pirates of the Asteroids
Lucky Starr and the Rings of Saturn
David Starr, Space Ranger
The Martian Way and Other Stories
The Naked Sun
Nightfall and Other Stories
Opus 100
Pebble in the Sky
The Rest of the Robots
The Stars, like Dust
A Whiff of Death

BALL, B. N.

Sundog

BALLARD, J. G.

Billenium
The Drowned World
Terminal Beach
Vermillion Sands
The Wind from Nowhere

BALMER, EDWIN, and PHILIP WYLIE

When Worlds Collide
After Worlds Collide

BEAGLE, PETER

The Last Unicorn

BESTER, ALFRED

The Demolished Man
The Stars My Destination

BIGGLE, LLOYD JR.

All the Colors of Darkness
The Light That Never Was
The Still, Small Voice of Trumpets
The World Menders

BLISH, JAMES

Black Easter; or, Faust Aleph Null
A Case of Conscience
Cities in Flight
A Life for the Stars
They Shall Have Stars
Earthman Come Home
The Triumph of Time
Midsummer Century
The Seedling Stars
A Torrent of Faces (with NORMAN KNIGHT)
Vor
The Warriors of Day

BOUCHER, ANTHONY

The Compleat Werewolf

BOYD, JOHN

The Last Starship from Earth
The Organ Bank Farm

BRADBURY, RAY

Fahrenheit 451
The Martian Chronicles

BRUNNER, JOHN

Catch a Falling Star
The Dramaturges of Yan
The Dreaming Earth
The Jagged Orbit
Stand on Zanzibar
Times Without Number
The Traveler in Black

BURGESS, ANTHONY

A Clockwork Orange
The Wanting Seed

BURROUGHS, EDGAR RICE

The Chessmen of Mars
A Fighting Man of Mars
John Carter of Mars
The Master Mind of Mars
The Moon Men
Thuvia, Maid of Mars
The Warlord of Mars

CAMPBELL, JOHN W.

Cloak of Aesir

CAPEK, KAREL

RUR (drama)
War with the Newts

CARTER, LIN

Outworlder

CHALMERS, ROBERT W.

The King in Yellow

CHANDLER, A. BERTRAM

Alternate Orbits/The Dark Dimension
Into the Alternate Universe
The Road to the Rim
The Sea Beasts

CHANT, JOY

Red Moon and Black Mountain

CHRISTOPHER, JOHN

No Blade of Grass
The Ragged Edge

CLARKE, ARTHUR C.

Childhood's End
The City and the Stars
A Fall of Moondust
The Other Side of the Sky
2001: A Space Odyssey
Tales From the White Hart
Tales of Ten Worlds
Voices from the Sky

CLEMENT, HAL

Ice World
Needle

Mission of Gravity
Space Lash
Starlight

CLIFTON, MARK, and FRANK RILEY

They'd Rather Be Right

CRICHTON, MICHAEL

The Andromeda Strain
Terminal Man

DAVIDSON, AVRAM

The Phoenix and the Mirror

DECAMP, L. SPRAGUE

The Castle of Iron (with FLETCHER PRATT)
The Goblin Tower
The Incomplete Enchanter (with FLETCHER PRATT)
Lest Darkness Fall

DELANY, SAMUEL R.

Babel-17
The Ballad of Beta-2
The Einstein Intersection
The Fall of the Towers
The Jewels of Aptor
Nova

DEL REY, LESTER

The 11th Commandment
Nerves
Pstalemate

DICK, PHILLIP K.

Clans of the Alphane Moon
The Crack in Space
The Man in the High Castle
A Maze of Death
Vulcan's Hammer

DICKSON, GORDON R.

The Alien Way
The Genetic General
Hour of the Horde
None But Man
No Room for Man
Soldier, Ask Not
Spacepaw
Tactics of Mistake
Wolfling

DOYLE, SIR ARTHUR CONAN

The Poison Belt

LORD DUNSANY

The King of Elfland's Daughter

ELLISON, HARLAN

Again Dangerous Visions
Dangerous Visions
I Have No Mouth and I Must Scream
Paingod

FARMER, PHILIP JOSÉ

Behind the Walls of Terra
The Fabulous Riverboat

HEINLEIN, ROBERT A.

Assignment in Eternity
Between Planets
Beyond This Horizon
Citizen of the Galaxy
The Day After Tomorrow
The Door into Summer
Double Star
Farmer in the Sky
Farnham's Freehold
Glory Road
The Green Hills of Earth
Have Space Suit—Will Travel
I Will Fear No Evil
The Man Who Sold the Moon
Methuselah's Children
The Moon is a Harsh Mistress
Orphans of the Sky
The Past Through Tomorrow
Podkayne of Mars
The Puppet Masters
Red Planet
Revolt in 2100
Rocket Ship Galileo
The Rolling Stones
6 × H
The Star Beast
Starman Jones
Starship Troopers
Stranger in a Strange Land
Time for the Stars
Tomorrow, the Stars
Tunnel in the Sky
Waldo & Magic, Incorporated

KEYES, DANIEL

Flowers for Algernon

KNIGHT, DAMON

Beyond the Barrier
Hell's Pavement

KUTTNER, HENRY

Fury
The Mask of Circe
Mutant

LAFFERTY, R. A.

Arrive at Easterwine
Fourth Mansions
Nine Hundred Grandmothers
The Reefs of Earth
Space Chantey

LAUMER, KEITH

Assignment in Nowhere
The Big Show
Dinosaur Beach
Envoy to New World
Galactic Diplomat
Galactic Odyssey
Graylon
The Great Time Machine Hoax
The Long Twilight
Nine by Laumer
A Plague of Demons
Planet Run (with GORDON R. DICKSON)

LEWIS, C. S.

Out of the Silent Planet
Perelandra
That Hideous Strength

LOVECRAFT, H. P.

The Color Out of Space

McCAFFREY, ANNE

Decision at Doona
Dragonflight
The Ship Who Sang

MacDONALD, JOHN D.

Wine of the Dreamers

McINTOSH, J. T.

The Rule of the Pagbeasts
Transmigration

McLAUGHLIN, DEAN

Dome World

MATHESON, RICHARD

I am Legend

MILLER, WALTER M. JR.

A Canticle for Leibowitz
A View from the Stars

MOORCOCK, MICHAEL

Behold the Man
The Black Corridor
The Dreaming City
The Knight of Swords
The Sleeping Sorceress
Stealer of Souls
Stormbringer

NIVEN, LARRY

All the Myriad Ways
A Gift from Earth
Neutron Star
Ringworld
The Shape of Space
World of Ptavvs

NOLAN, WILLIAM F.

Logan's Run (with GEORGE CLAYTON JOHNSON)
The Pseudo-People
A Wilderness of Stars

NORTON, ANDRE

The Beast Master
Breed to Come
Catseye
Dark Piper
Daybreak—2250 A.D.
The Defiant Agents
Dragon Magic
Dread Companion
Exiles of the Stars
Galactic Derelict

Star Surgeon

NOWLAN, PHILIP FRANCIS

Armageddon 2419 A.D.

OLIVER, CHAD

Shadows in the Sun

ORWELL, GEORGE

1984

PANGBORN, EDGAR

Davy
West of the Sun

PANSHIN, ALEXEI

Masque World
Rite of Passage
Star Well
The Thurb Revolution

POHL, FREDERICK

The Age of the Pussyfoot
Alternating Currents
Drunkard's Walk
Gladiator-at Law (with C. M. KORNBLUTH)
Gravy Planet (with C. M. K.)
A Plague of Pythons
Rogue Star (with JACK WILLIAMSON)
Search the Sky (with C. M. K.)
Slave Ship
The Space Merchants (with C. M. K.)

Tomorrow Times Seven
Wolfbane (with C. M. K.)

PRATT, FLETCHER

The Blue Star
The Well of the Unicorn

REYNOLDS, MACK

After Some Tomorrow

RUSS, JOANNA

And Chaos Died

RUSSELL, ERIC FRANK

The Great Explosion
Men, Martians, and Machines
Wasp

SABERHAGEN, FRED

Berserker
The Black Mountains
The Broken Lands

SCHMITZ, JAMES H.

The Demon Breed
The Lion Game
The Witches of Karres

SHAW, BOB

Other Days, Other Eyes

SILVERBERG, ROBERT

Earthmen and Strangers (ed.)
Hawksbill Station
The Man in the Maze
The Mirror of Infinity (ed.)
Nightwings
Parsecs and Parables
Science Fiction Hall of Fame, Vol. I (ed.)
Thorns
Those Who Watch
A Time of Changes
To Open the Sky
Tower of Glass

SIMAK, CLIFFORD D.

City
Destiny Doll
The Goblin Reservation
Out of Their Minds
Ring Around the Sun
Time and Again
Way Station
The Werewolf Principle

SMITH, CORDWAINER

The Planet Buyer
Space Lords
Stardreamer
The Underpeople
You'll Never Be the Same

SMITH, E. E. "DOC"

Children of the Lens
First Lensman

Galactic Patrol
Gray Lensman
Masters of the Vortex
Second Stage Lensmen
Skylark Duquesne
The Skylark of Space
Skylark Three
Skylark of Valeron
Triplanetary

SPINRAD, NORMAN

Bug Jack Barron
The Last Hurrah of the Golden Horde

STAPLEDON, OLAF

Last and First Men
Odd John
Starmaker

STASHEFF, CHRISTOPHER

King Kobold
The Warlock in Spite of Himself

STURGEON, THEODORE

E Pluribus Unicorn
More Than Human
Some of Your Blood
The Synthetic Man
Venus Plus X

SWANN, THOMAS BURNETT

The Dolphin and the Deep

TENN, WILLIAM

A Lamp for Medusa
The Wooden Star

TOLKIEN, J. R. R.

The Hobbit
The Ring Trilogy
    The Fellowship of the Ring
    The Two Towers
    The Return of the Ring
The Tolkien Reader

TRIMBLE, L. and J.

Guardians of the Gate

TUCKER, WILSON

The Year of the Quiet Sun

VANCE, JACK

The Dragon Masters/The Last Castle
The Dying Earth
The Languages of Pao

VAN VOGT, A. E.

Destination: Universe
Empire of the Atom
Mission to the Stars
More Than Superhuman
Planets for Sale (with E. MAYNE HULL)
Slan
The War Against the Rull

The Weapon Shops of Isher
The Winged Man (with E. M. H.)
The World of Null A
The Pawns of Null A

VERNE, JULES

Journey to the Center of the Earth
20,000 Leagues Under the Sea

VON HARBOW, THEA

Metropolis

VONNEGUT, KURT, JR.

Breakfast of Champions
Cat's Cradle
God Bless You, Mr. Rosewater
Mother Night
Player Piano
The Sirens of Titan
Slaughterhouse Five
Welcome to the Monkey House

WALTON, EVANGELINE

Witch House

WEINBAUM, STANLEY

The Black Flame
A Martian Odyssey
The New Adam

WELLS, H. G.

The First Men in the Moon

The Time Machine
The War of the Worlds

WHITE, T. E.

The Once and Future King

WHITE, TED

The Sorceress of Qar

WILLIAMSON, JACK

Dragon's Island

WYLIE, PHILLIP

The Disappearance

WYNDHAM, JOHN

The Day of the Triffids
The Kraken Wakes
The Midwich Cuckoos
Rebirth

ZEBROWSKI, GEORGE

The Omega Point

ZELAZNY, ROGER

Creatures of Light and Darkness
The Dream Master
The Guns of Avalon
Isle of the Dead
Jack of Shadows

Lord of Light
Nine Princes in Amber
This Immortal
Today We Choose Faces

A Selected Bibliography of Works About Science Fiction

Amis, Kingsley. *New Maps of Hell: A Survey of Science Fiction.* New York: Harcourt, Brace, 1960. Examines science fiction as an instrument of social criticism.

Atheling, William, Jr. [pseud. for James Blish]. *The Issue at Hand.* Chicago: Advent, 1964. A solid collection of critical reviews of science fiction which appeared, for the most part, in science fiction magazines.

————. *More Issues at Hand.* Chicago: Advent, 1970. Much like its predecessor, this one deals with later work and leans more toward longer works.

Bailey, J. O. *Pilgrims Through Space and Time.* New York: Argus Books, 1947. One of the classics in the study of science fiction from a historical point-of-view. (2nd. ed., 1972)

Bretnor, Reginald, ed. *Modern Science Fiction: Its Meaning and Future.* New York: Coward-McCann, 1953. Dealing with the themes of science fiction mostly, this is a collection of essays by science fiction writers and editors.

Clareson, Thomas D., ed. *SF: The Other Side of Realism.* Bowling Green, Ohio: Bowling Green

University Popular Press, 1971. An excellent anthology of science fiction criticism, the first of its kind.

DAVENPORT, BASIL, ed. *The Science Fiction Novel: Imagination and Social Criticism.* Chicago: Advent, 1959. Talks by four science fiction writers about science fiction as social criticism; the assessments are divergent.

ESBACH, LLOYD, ed. *Of Worlds Beyond: The Science of Science Fiction Writing.* Chicago: Advent, 1964. Intended for would-be writers, this is a collection of how-to-do-it essays, each on a different aspect, by science fiction writers and editors.

KNIGHT, DAMON. *In Search of Wonder.* Chicago: Advent, 1967 (2nd ed.). A series of reviews and studies of science fiction as literature.

LUNDWALL, SAM. *Science Fiction: What It's All About.* New York: Ace Books, 1971. A survey of the field that may serve as a starting point, but little more.

MOSKOWITZ, SAM. *Explorers of the Infinite: Shapers of Science Fiction.* Cleveland and New York: World, 1963. A historical view of science fiction concentrating on the early years.

———. *Seekers of Tomorrow: Masters of Modern Science Fiction.* Cleveland and New York: World, 1966. A continuation, in the same vein, of *Explorers of the Infinite.*

———. *Science Fiction by Gaslight: A History and Anthology of Science Fiction in the Popular Magazines 1891-1911.* Cleveland and New York: World, 1968. The title says it all.

———. *Under the Moons of Mars: A History and Anthology of "The Scientific Romance" in the Munsey Magazines, 1912-1920.* New York: Holt, Rinehart, and Winston, 1970. Once again, the title tells what it does. The work of Moskowitz is important because he is thorough and because of the comprehensiveness of his enterprise.

PANSHIN, ALEXEI. *Heinlein in Dimension.* Chicago: Advent, 1969. An interesting overview of Heinlein's work, presenting both his weaknesses and strengths, and evaluating his influence.

WOLLHEIM, DONALD A. *The Universe Makers: Science Fiction Today.* New York: Harper & Row, 1971. A personalized history-reminiscence-reaction to science fiction from a man whose entire life has been involved with science fiction.

Those who wish to pursue the study of science fiction further should by all means consult, if not buy, the following bibliography:

CLARESON, THOMAS D. *Science Fiction Criticism: An Annotated Checklist.* Kent, Ohio: The Kent State University Press, 1972. The bibliography is extensive and quite up to date; the annotations are very helpful, as are the divisions into which the works are divided. A necessary research tool for science fiction study and criticism.

Index

296

297